NA 737 .H39 C78 1994

Cruikshank, Jeffrey L.

Herman Miller, Inc.,
   buildings and beliefs

DATE DUE

Herman Miller, Inc.: Buildings and Beliefs

MARIANNE JEWELL MEMORIAL LIBRARY
BAKER COLLEGE OF MUSKEGON
MUSKEGON, MICHIGAN 49442

© 1994 Jeffrey L. Cruikshank and Clark Malcolm
All rights reserved.

First published in the United States in 1994 by
The American Institute of Architects Press
1735 New York Avenue, N.W., Washington, D.C. 20006

Library of Congress Cataloging-in-Publication Data

Cruikshank, Jeffrey L.
  Herman Miller, Inc., buildings and beliefs /
  Jeffrey L. Cruikshank and Clark Malcolm.
  176 p.   21 x 29.7 cm.
  Includes bibliographical references and index.
  ISBN 1-55835-132-9
  1. Herman Miller (Firm) 2. Architectural services marketing—
United States. 3. Architectural services marketing—England.
4. Corporate image—United States. 5. Corporate image—
England.
I. Malcolm, Clark. II. Title.
NA737.H39C78 1994   94-41534
720'.92'2—dc20   CIP

Printed and bound in Hong Kong
through Palace Press International, San Francisco

Designed by Judy Kohn
Kohn Cruikshank Inc, Boston

Herman Miller, Inc.: Buildings and Beliefs

Jeffrey L. Cruikshank
and
Clark Malcolm

The American Institute of Architects Press
Washington, D.C.

To architects and other teachers, who can never really know where their influence ends

Acknowledgements

A book like this happens only because lots of people are far too generous with their time and thoughts.

Several of Herman Miller's designer-teachers come first to mind: Jeff Scherer, Mack Scogin, Nick Grimshaw and Neven Sidor, Bill Stumpf, and Bob Petras and his Heery & Heery colleagues. We are also happy to include in this select company Elaine K. Sewell Jones, wife of the late A. Quincy Jones, recently elected to the American Institute of Architects for her many contributions to the field.

Hugh De Pree, Max De Pree, Gord Nagelkirk, Tom Pratt, Kathy Pruden, Dick Ruch, John Stivers, Phil Strengholt, and Tom Wolterink gave us inside perspectives that lend our tale the ring of truth.

Linda Folland and Barbara Hire, managers of Herman Miller's extensive archives, produced the written record and also processed our interviews. Tomorrow's researchers will be in their debt, as we have been. Rich Rutledge helped immensely in collecting illustrations.

John Berry, Ralph Caplan, Max De Pree, Marty Dugan, Steve Frykholm, Elaine Jones, Gord Nagelkirk, and John Stivers reviewed early drafts of the manuscript; Bernie Van't Hul and Betty Hahn scrutinized the final draft with special care. Janet Rumbarger at the AIA Press shepherded the book through production.

Ann Cruikshank and Judy Malcolm accepted our frequent absences with cheerful resignation, although both were skeptical about the UK trip. Thank you; and thanks, too, to Russell, Ben, Meredith, and Alice for letting us bear down on this (most of the time).

Finally, special thanks to Rolf Fehlbaum, who has lived through some of the knotty issues described in these pages and nevertheless consented to write a foreword. That was a special favor, and we appreciate it.

Jeff Cruikshank, Boston
Clark Malcolm, Ann Arbor

Contents

Foreword

Most books about architecture are written for architects. *Herman Miller, Inc.: Buildings and Beliefs* should be read by anybody planning to build a building. It is not a theoretical thesis about corporate architecture. It is a practical book that will help any organization do a better building by stimulating thinking about "space for people at work." In so doing, it will create more value for the organization and for the environment. A pleasant bonus is the charming storytelling about the culture of an interesting company—Herman Miller, Inc.

The Herman Miller experience is valuable in many aspects. I find it especially instructive because the story is not intimidating— not a story we can only admire from a distance but never achieve for ourselves, like the cooperation between Rathenau and Behrens in the case of AEG in Berlin around the beginning of this century.

The story of Herman Miller's architecture is the result of decent people caring about the environment and applying to architecture the lessons they learned in designing products. Because the people at Herman Miller were more outspoken than possibly any other corporation and they documented their thoughts, we can now learn from their experience. If only for the different guidelines for architecture, this book is an important resource.

It surprises me that the idea of taking architecture seriously and making it an important component of corporate culture is rare. There are a few examples in addition to Herman Miller—AEG in Berlin, Olivetti in Ivrea, and Cummins Engine in Columbus—but not many. Except for the case of AEG, little about the architect-client relationship is documented well.

Of course there are companies that put up great buildings on highly visible sites. But that is not what this book is about. This book concerns an attitude *vis à vis* architecture and building, an attitude that to my knowledge has not been expressed and realized with such consequence over decades by any other sizable corporation.

The result of the lack of such an attitude is the disastrous state of industrial sites all over the world. It is difficult to say which is worse: the total neglect of the issue or a reliance on the pretentious cliché that architecture is chosen for particular sites.

I can illustrate from my own experience how much one can learn from Herman Miller. In the beginning of the 1980s, Vitra, the company I head, started an initiative that resulted in an architectural campus in southern Germany with buildings by Grimshaw, Siza, Gehry, Ando, and Zaha Adid. I would never have developed the idea or the confidence to carry through with it had it not been for my exposure to the thinking of Herman Miller, which started in the late 1950s when Vitra became the European licensee for Herman Miller's products. I learned a great deal from George Nelson (whose importance may still not be appreciated sufficiently), Charles and Ray Eames, the De Pree family, and many others at Herman Miller. I learned especially from Max De Pree, who has the unique ability to combine thinking, doing, and teaching. Some of these lessons were:

◆ Every building—even the smallest addition—is an opportunity, not simply a necessity. Later I understood that to treat every building in this way is an obligation, because a building belongs to the public. Architecture for the workplace is so important because people spend so much of their lives there. Sadly, we often work at unattractive sites in uninspiring environments. Who else can take over the cultural role of client that was played by royalty, the aristocracy, and the enlightened bourgeoisie if not modern-day corporations?

◆ An architect does not simply provide a service. He or she is a partner in a joint effort. It is mandatory for clients to spend enough time to find a gifted architect sharing the same values. It is equally important to listen to and trust an architect. Working with an architect can be a real learning experience.

◆ An architect needs support from the most powerful people (or at least one of them) in an organization throughout the process. The building in the end may not be the same building you imagined in the beginning. If you are a good partner, the result will be more than you can imagine.

◆ Architecture for a corporation is not a power trip for executives. It should first uplift and inspire the people who work there, and it should be fun for visitors and an asset for the community. I have also learned that corporations should allow architectural pluralism and approach each site and purpose with an open mind.

◆ Good architecture yields results far beyond your efforts, results only partly expressible in the business logic of productivity and public relations. If some of the rewards of pursuing good architecture do not make the list of standard business objectives, something is wrong with the list.

◆ Finally, by looking at a building project as an opportunity, it is not difficult and not costly at all to realize something far better than you will by looking at architecture as a necessity.

I have learned these lessons by experience, and now they are all in this book. Had I read this book years ago, my learning would have been much easier. My hope is that many people involved in the process of building buildings will read this book, understand their opportunities and obligations, and realize that they, too, can gain from preparing themselves as clients.

Rolf Fehlbaum
Chairman and CEO
Vitra, Switzerland

Herman Miller, Inc.: Buildings and Beliefs

What's important?

This book is about architecture, but only indirectly. More immediately, it is about how one company answers seven questions about people and spaces. Sometimes the answers lead to architecture.

This book doesn't tell companies how to build buildings. Instead, it tries to help people and companies think about space for people at work. It does so by explaining how one company, Herman Miller, Inc., builds relationships with its architects. Then come bricks and mortar.

In 1923, D.J. De Pree bought Star Furniture Company in Zeeland, Michigan, with financial help from his father-in-law, Herman Miller, a man known in the community for his honesty and forthrightness. De Pree renamed the company, which has since grown to a billion-dollar, publicly owned manufacturer of furniture for offices and other work environments.

As we looked into the company's building projects and its relationships with architects, the accumulated stories and experiences seemed to coalesce around the seven questions that have become our chapter titles.

Why focus on this Michigan-based manufacturer of furniture and systems for office environments?

First, because Herman Miller works hard—perhaps harder than most companies—at keeping its philosophical house in order. Beginning with its founder, D.J. De Pree, Herman Miller has made a point of discussing, arguing about (even agonizing over), and writing down what it believes and how it should behave. The company, we believe, is a good example of how trying to arrive at a clear idea of what an organization is about—what its values and goals are—can help that organization build better, more humane buildings. The early chapters of this book, therefore, will focus on Herman Miller's philosophy about its employees and its customers; the later chapters will explain how that philosophy has been expressed in architecture.

Second, Herman Miller has for more than six decades designed and manufactured a range of products intended to make places for people more livable and functional. The company has produced some of the most admired home and office furnishings of the 20th century. By engaging such designers as Gilbert Rohde, George Nelson, Charles Eames, Alexander Girard, Robert Propst, and Bill Stumpf, the company has achieved a reputation for leadership and innovation in design. Over the years, Herman Miller has learned to work productively with designers and others outside the company, who in turn have been attuned to the talents and needs of architects. (Many architects specify Herman Miller products for use in the facilities they design.) The company has been a good student.

Alexander Girard,
George Nelson,
D.J. De Pree, Ray and
Charles Eames

And the boundary between industrial design and architectural design has been crossed at many points in the company's history. Both disciplines, as well as Herman Miller, have benefited.

George Nelson's long affiliation with the company is only one example. Nelson, a registered architect and managing editor of *Architectural Forum,* was retained by Herman Miller in 1945 as an industrial designer. In subsequent years, he conceived of many of Herman Miller's products, and his office created the corporate logo. Along with his architect partner Gordon Chadwick, Nelson also designed the first three buildings (built in five increments) in Herman Miller's corporate headquarters complex in Zeeland, Michigan.

Third, Herman Miller has acquired three decades of experience in the building and rebuilding of various work-related spaces: offices, manufacturing facilities, warehouses, research facilities, and showrooms. The company's spectacular growth in the 1970s and 1980s led to facilities in different regions of the US and overseas. The company has learned a great deal from these experiences.

Fourth, Herman Miller is recognized as a good place to work.[1] This reputation in part grows out of the quality of the spaces within which Herman Miller people do their jobs.

"How people feel about their work place affects their morale and in turn their productivity," as the master plan for one of Herman Miller's buildings puts it. "If we think of factory/office complexes as large, dull, strictly utilitarian structures, we fail to provide for the human spirit. Brightening the human experience and enhancing the environment is appropriate. The work place should express a certain joy and embody enthusiasm."[2]

"The work place should express a certain joy and embody enthusiasm."

Other companies have built more buildings than Herman Miller. Few have so persistently and often successfully focused on getting its work spaces right. With one exception, the company still occupies all the buildings it has built for itself. Several of Herman Miller's individual facilities have been singled out for praise, and the company's portfolio of buildings is a distinguished one. In 1981, for example, Herman Miller received a special award from the American Institute of Architects for inspiring and influencing the architectural profession.[3]

Of course, none of Herman Miller's buildings is flawless. The company has made an effort to understand and learn from its mistakes. Where possible, it has tried to share what it has learned with other companies.

This book, in fact, grows out of those two continuing efforts: to learn from history and to make learned lessons public.

Why does architecture matter?

Before we set out to answer this chapter's question—*What's important?*—we should take a look at the larger context. Is corporate architecture worth worrying about?

For those measuring the national economy, the answer is clearly yes. Currently, money spent on new construction and renovation is approaching a half-trillion dollars annually, or more than 8 percent of the US gross national product.[4]

For those holding corporate purse strings, the answer is also yes. Even in an era of downsizing, new corporate facilities represent a large proportion of capital investment. Each year, the nation's corporations begin construction projects worth billions of dollars. The largest of these projects can create, collectively, millions of square feet of work-related space.[5]

For architects, of course, the answer is emphatically affirmative. Design for commercial clients is by far the largest source of architectural billings (59 percent in 1990).[6] Office buildings are the single largest source of architectural fees, accounting for 15 percent of revenues in recent years.[7] Warehouses and other relatively simple commercial structures are among the most profitable buildings that architects design.

Finally, if the *users* of all those buildings were consulted, they would no doubt rank the quality of corporate architecture high on their list of what's important. According to recent studies, not many of those people who spend many of their waking hours in commercial buildings are happy about the buildings they occupy. Some 30 million US workers work in offices, spending 90 percent of their time in controlled environments. According to one author, 70 percent of them are fundamentally unhappy with their workplaces.[8]

Such numbers begin to get at the heart of a complicated question. Can an affordable, fully functional, and fully flexible building really inspire people and encourage them to be productive?

Frank Gehry, who designed Herman Miller's manufacturing facility in Sacramento in the late 1980s, takes the question seriously and describes how his interests and Herman Miller's interests converged on a subject that mattered very much to both parties. "You shouldn't make people feel less than they are," says Gehry. "The space should enhance them, instead of detracting from them. It should be uplifting, instructive, positive. They have the right to the best I can do as an architect—maybe even a little more so, because it's a factory, and people don't usually hire architects to do factories."

Why do it? Because, according to Herman Miller, good architecture matters.

According to recent studies, not many of those people who spend many of their waking hours in commercial buildings are happy about the buildings they occupy.

Merely to say so is easy. But how a company acts is the difficult and
important thing. By all accounts, Herman Miller is a company that acts on
its beliefs about architecture. "If you *say* you respect individuals," as one
Herman Miller manager puts it, "your buildings had better show it. If a
company says it believes in the value of each person, its production employees had better be able to wash up and eat in facilities as well appointed
as any. And if you say that the work environment can help organizations be
more productive, then your own environment had better do exactly that."

"Some years ago," says Max De Pree, former chief executive officer of
Herman Miller, "in one of our regular employee surveys, we asked a question about what made people apply to Herman Miller. Something like
70 percent said that they decided to apply because of the way the buildings
looked." That tradition continues with the company's most recent buildings. "It's a facility that you hear people in the Holland/Zeeland area
talking about," says Martin Dugan, vice president of Facility Management,
about Herman Miller's recently completed Design Yard, "and wishing
they could work there." [9]

Max De Pree

A good work environment can transform a company's workers into an
auxiliary sales force. One day in 1986, Max De Pree paid a call on the
facilities manager of an Oakland, California, bank that had recently made
a large purchase of Herman Miller products. "Max," said the manager,
"I don't want to put down the abilities of your salesmen, because they
were excellent, but what made up my mind was when I was in your chair
plant in Holland, and I spent a lot of time talking to the woman who
assembles the chairs.

"I felt, after talking to her," the manager continued, "that if a company has
this kind of person assembling its chairs, then it's the kind of company
I want to do business with." [10]

The chair assembler spoke her mind in a workplace designed to satisfy,
support, and involve its occupants. "The design concept," wrote the
architect of the chair plant, "and particularly the 'people' orientation of the
project, is not an architectural concept, it's a Herman Miller concept . . . .
The quality of this project will reflect not only the product quality
of Herman Miller's chairs, but more importantly, the quality of Herman
Miller people." [11]

"Quality" has become an overworked word. "Almost every company insists
that their goal is to achieve excellent quality," says Hugh De Pree, who
preceded his brother Max as Herman Miller's chief executive officer. "Well,
if that's true, then certainly their architecture ought to reflect that. It ought
to say, 'Look, this is something we are *proud* of. We are proud to be in
this building. We are proud to have good people here. This is evidence that

we are doing something for the people who work here. This is evidence that we make 'good goods.'"

In Herman Miller's eyes, only people literate about the business and intimate with their own jobs can make their organization succeed. Good architecture matters because it helps people do their best work. It matters because, in the words of the late William Caudill, an architect and longtime member of the company's board, the best architecture provides for the physical, emotional, and intellectual needs of people who experience it.

Nine facilities

The April 1959 issue of *Fortune* magazine included an article on the "100 Best Designed, Mass-Produced Products of Modern Times," as selected by distinguished designers, architects, and design teachers from around the world. Out in Zeeland, Michigan, a small furniture company celebrated.

"We at Herman Miller are very proud that, of the 100 items listed, four products are Herman Miller's," an internal company newsletter noted the following month. "Listed as the second best designed product is the Eames molded plywood chair. The Eames plastic chair is number 32, the Nelson Storage Wall number 54, and the Eames 670 and 671 [lounge] chair and ottoman are number 67 in the selection."

Also included in the selection were the "Ball Clock" and bubble lamps designed by George Nelson and produced by the Howard Miller Clock Company, now across the street from Herman Miller's Main Site in Zeeland. "It is significant to note," the newsletter continued, "that of the 100 best products, six are manufactured right here in Zeeland. No other small city can come anywhere near this distinction in the selection."

When the *Fortune* article appeared, George Nelson was hard at work on a new Herman Miller project. In collaboration with his architectural partner Gordon Chadwick, Nelson was designing a second building at Herman Miller's headquarters, in the small city of Zeeland.

The Zeeland site was the first of nine that the company was to invest in during the next three decades. Each of those nine sites is described in illustrated sections in this book. As we try to answer the seven questions that Herman Miller's people and experiences have led us to, we draw upon the stories of these nine sites.

Good architecture matters because it helps people do their best work.

The best architecture provides for the physical, emotional, and intellectual needs of people who experience it.

What's important?

In the summer of 1960, while George Nelson and Gordon Chadwick were designing the Zeeland facility that became known as the Main Site, Herman Miller's 362 employees were going about their business: manufacturing, assembling, transporting, displaying, and selling high-quality furniture for the home and office.

On one of those summer days, someone on the company's small management team was struck by an article he read in an out-of-town newspaper. The result was a short editorial in the next issue of the *Herman Miller Memo,* a motivational newsletter sent out every other month to the company's dealers.

"An article appearing in the Real Estate Section of the *New York Times* caught our eye the other day," wrote the anonymous author. "Bearing the headline 'Today's Outstanding Contemporary Buildings Reflect the Corporate Image,' this article goes on to report how more and more businesses are learning that good design pays off. The author, Thomas W. Ennis, says, 'The idea that good architecture is good business is becoming axiomatic in corporate management circles . . . . The buildings in many cases are regarded as community assets, and as such their public relations value is beyond reckoning in dollars. Business is given a boost too, and so is company morale.'" [12]

With the benefit of 30 years' hindsight—and companies like IBM, Olivetti, and Cummins Engine notwithstanding—it appears that the *Times* writer's interpretation was too rosy. Having an Eliot Noyes serving as IBM's architectural "conscience" remained the rare exception; a focus on good architecture did not become axiomatic in corporate management circles. In subsequent decades, good architecture has lost ground in the corporate setting.

For a number of reasons, many corporations (occasionally even Herman Miller) have lost sight of the value of building good buildings. They lost sight of the cohesiveness of vision presented by a combination such as Nelson, Eames, and Girard; they succumbed to fragmented problem-solving. In the name of energy efficiency, for example, many companies downgraded the quality of the work environment. Even those companies that defended the quality of the work environment—in terms of air quality and climate controls, for example—did so mainly to satisfy the environmental needs of their computers.

A review of current books and articles about good management is not encouraging. In most of them, corporate architecture doesn't even register as an issue. Many experts on management exhort companies to "empower" the workforce, and many argue for a safe and clean workplace, logically organized. Few argue for an *inspiring* workplace. Even people who have studied Herman Miller, and who have applauded the company's efforts to create "covenantal" relationships with its workers, have mainly missed a key point: that a consistent focus on good architecture is an integral part of that covenant and Herman Miller's philosophy.

Architects share some of the blame for the decline in corporate architecture. In recent years, even among leaders of the architectural profession, a concern for the needs of building occupants has taken a back seat to styling. Issues of function and appropriateness have been subordinated to what architect and planner Moshe Safdie, echoing others before him, has called "architecture as sculpture."[13]

Despite these trends, there may be grounds to be optimistic about the future of corporate architecture. For a number of reasons, both pragmatic and idealistic, the needs of the worker seem to be coming once again to the fore.

For instance: Today's managers are beginning to think differently about investments in architecture. Recent studies have shown that when considered over a 40-year life cycle, the *least* significant costs of a building are the upfront costs of site acquisition, design, and construction (in the range of 2 to 3 percent). The most significant are the salaries and benefits of the people who work within it (90 to 92 percent).[14] When presented with these kinds of numbers, many managers think differently about the real costs of a building's shortcomings.

For example, the annual cost of bad indoor air quality to the US economy has been estimated at $75 billion.[15] The annual cost of workplace-related stress and sickness exceeds $450 billion. Corporations under increasing competitive pressures, and the architects who design for them, are beginning to take heed. "The typical postwar American office tower," notes *Architectural Record,* "with its enormous floor plates and hermetically sealed windows, is becoming obsolete, replaced by more user-friendly structures that save money, promote productivity, conserve natural resources, and allow employees some control over their environment."[16]

Governments, too, are responding. In the US, ventilation standards that were lowered in the wake of the 1973 oil embargo—and which have been blamed for the recent emergence of "sick-building syndrome"—have been raised again, in some cases dramatically. Several countries in Northern Europe have passed legislation requiring functional windows in the workplace and stipulating the maximum allowable distance between a worker and the nearest window.[17]

With a sense of guarded optimism about the future of commercial buildings, therefore, let us return to the question with which we opened this chapter. When it comes to corporate architecture, *What's important?*

It's important for the corporation to figure out what it's all about, to know its place under the sun. This is the particular focus of the next chapter: *Who are we?*

It's important to figure out what the corporation needs to learn, and who can best teach it. If architecture is indeed needed, then it's vitally important to pick an architect who can teach. This is the subject of Chapter 3: *Who can teach us something?*

If architecture is indeed needed, then it's vitally important to pick an architect who can teach.

It's important to identify the corporation's opportunities and (probably even more important) its constraints and obligations. This is a commonly posed challenge, of course, but not commonly posed in the context of architecture.

"We recently heard of a man who had made a good deal of money all of a sudden, and who subsequently let his sense of values get a little dim," wrote D.J. De Pree in 1948. "He bought a big rundown estate and got busy with a flourish to fix it up. He took a Swedish stone mason to look over the job and told him to proceed to do anything that ought to be done. 'Money is no object,' said the owner. The next day, the stone mason sent word that he didn't want to do the work. He said, 'There's no fun in a job where you can't spend time figuring out ways to save money.'"[18]

An awareness of the financial costs of architecture is important at Herman Miller. "The biggest problem that I had with architects," recalls former Herman Miller vice president Tom Wolterink, "is that they always dreamed of having Herman Miller as an account. They equated that with unlimited budget—whereas in reality, Herman Miller was run by Dutchmen, who were very thrifty. Cost constraints were never far away."

In addition to budget, other less tangible and even more important obligations must be acknowledged. "Once a building is up," says Max De Pree, "it's publicly owned. It's there. We can't avoid seeing it. So it either blesses us or embarrasses us. People who build buildings don't have the right to behave only in their own interest. A building is either an environmental asset or an environmental problem."

Or, as architect Quincy Jones liked to put it, "There is no unimportant architecture."

"There is no unimportant architecture."

Constraints and obligations are the subject of Chapter 4: *What do we owe?*

It's important for the corporation and architect to build a productive working relationship. Of course, corporations and architects have been coexisting—and even cooperating—for centuries, and their relationships have produced many buildings. What needs constant rediscovery is the fact that the quality of a building is directly related to the quality of the relationship between the client and the architect.

This is one thing of which Herman Miller is sure. As Max De Pree comments, "Nick Grimshaw told the Royal Institute of British Architects one time that the quality of the Bath building, which won the Financial Times award as the best building in Great Britain, was directly related to the way the work was assigned. He said that the poetry of the brief made the building possible." Relationship-building and subsequent steps in the design and construction process are the subject of Chapter 5: *How do we get there from here?*

It's important to anticipate the detours and pitfalls that can surprise people as they put up a building—and also to understand what to do about them when they do appear. Chapter 6 addresses a difficult question: *What can go wrong?*

It's important to think of a good facility, in service to an evolving company, as a work-in-progress to be reviewed and revised over many decades. Occupants of a building must be allowed to improve it. There must be someone in the company who is willing and able to carry the torch for good architecture in an informed, compassionate, and hard-boiled way. Chapter 7 answers our last question: *What happens next?*

In 1961, D.J. De Pree set forth Herman Miller's rationale for building one of its first buildings. "It is quite evident," he wrote in a company newsletter, "that we are in the business of changing the environment of people, and we believe this is change for the better because it makes living cleaner, more orderly, simplified, restful, comfortable, healthier, and has a lot to do with freeing people for more worthwhile activity."[19]

But first, we might add, a corporation must get its buildings right.

The Main Site

In the late 1950s, Herman Miller had five small plants. Plant No.'s 1, 3, 4, and 5 in Zeeland, Michigan, made furniture, fabrics, and various special products; and Plant No.2 in Venice, California, manufactured the plastic chairs designed by Charles Eames. When it became clear that consolidating most of the existing plants would save money, and also that expansion was a strong possibility, the company purchased a 35-acre farm in Zeeland. The De Prees then asked Nelson—with Eames, one of the company's two product designers since the mid-1940s— to design a combined manufacturing-and-office facility.

George Nelson's plan

Herman Miller followed Nelson's five-building campus plan (sometimes faithfully, sometimes less so) over the next decade. In 1970, the company retained California architect A. Quincy Jones to develop a master plan for an expanded Main Site, and to make the overall work environment more cohesive. Major expansions and alterations to the Main Site continued for the next two decades. These included the construction of an Energy Center, a Computer Center, and the conversion of 88,000 square feet of manufacturing space to office space. Houston-based Caudill Rowlett Scott (CRS), and later the Minneapolis firm of Meyer, Scherer & Rockcastle, served as design consultants on the site after Jones's death in 1979. CRS began a conversion of pieces of the Main Site to office space in 1980; this process was continued, on a dramatic scale, by Meyer, Scherer & Rockcastle in the late 1980s.

Quincy Jones's plan

CRS plan

Interior architecture at the Zeeland site

Office area at Zeeland site

Meeting area at Zeeland site

Zeeland Main Site

Energy center and spine

Energy center

Elevated walkway at Zeeland site

A story about Herman Miller:

In 1948, designer Charles Eames proposed that one of his highly successful
plywood chairs, which Herman Miller had mass-produced for two
years, also be made out of a thermosetting resin reinforced with glass fibers.
Eames was convinced that new technologies for molding plastic would
finally allow him to achieve the results he wanted. If these new processes
worked, Herman Miller could make chairs in bright and permanent colors.
The chairs could be made stackable. Maybe most important, the price
could come down, so that more people could afford them.

Unfortunately, the company didn't have enough money to pay for the new
tools. Jim Eppinger, Herman Miller's legendary sales manager who established his reputation during the 1930s and 1940s, chipped in to help pay the
tooling costs, and the new Eames chairs went into production in 1949.
They were an immediate success.

"We were a Salvation Army operation," says Max De Pree, reflecting back
on this episode. "But we felt we were on a mission."

"Beginning next
Monday, the factories
in Zeeland will
operate without the
use of the time
clocks."

A second story about Herman Miller:

A new employee newsletter appeared in the Herman Miller factory
and offices in 1956. "Beginning next Monday," read a short article in the
December 6 issue of *Headlines*, "the factories in Zeeland will operate
without the use of the time clocks."

For record-keeping purposes, the article went on to say, employees would
have to fill out time cards at the beginning and end of their shifts. But
it would no longer be necessary to deal with the twice-daily irritations of
the time clock: arriving ten minutes early to punch in, and waiting
in line to punch out.

Chair designed
by Charles Eames

A third story:

Glenn Walters began his career with Herman Miller as a salesman. He
helped introduce Action Office in the late 1960s, and in 1980 he succeeded
Hugh De Pree as president of the company. One day, Max De Pree
(then chief executive officer) arrived early at work and came upon Walters
picking up beer cans in the parking lot at the Main Site.

"A normal part of the president's job," said Walters matter-of-factly.
"You pick up this garbage all the time."

De Pree knew exactly what Walters meant: "I close closet doors wherever I go. I can't explain why they're always left open. There's a janitor's closet next to our main entrance which is usually open. I always close it. I don't want a customer to come in here and have an open closet door be the first thing he or she sees."

A fourth and final story:

In 1990, Herman Miller's Zeeland-based employees set out to raise money to help a colleague undergoing an expensive medical treatment. They organized a walk-a-thon and began asking for pledges—so much per mile. One relatively new employee, with only a partial command of English, pledged several dollars per mile from his modest salary. The fundraisers were concerned. After some debate, they approached their generous colleague. Did he understand, they asked, that he had just pledged a fairly large percentage of his take-home pay for that week?

Of course he did, he replied with some indignation. He understood very well that Herman Miller was his family, and that the company and his coworkers had been generous to him when *he* had needed help. Now, he said, it was his turn.

Companies, legends, and architecture

In a book about corporations and architecture, why are these stories worth telling? Because they suggest how a corporation understands itself. Collectively, they describe the incidents that answer the question, "Who are we?" Self-awareness equips a company and its architects to understand the intangible qualities that need to be expressed in bricks and steel. Only with this knowledge—of the *character* of an organization—can an architect design a building that goes beyond the basics of providing shelter.

> Self-awareness equips a company and its architects to understand the intangible qualities that need to be expressed in bricks and steel.

"It's easier for companies who have their values down, and know themselves," says Robert Petras, a member of the Heery & Heery team that designed Herman Miller's Roswell, Georgia, facility. "If they don't, then you have to go through a period of education—a learning process. You have to help them identify their corporate values and understand their own philosophy. Good design is more difficult in that context."

But what *are* "values"? Can a corporation develop them, hold them, defend them? The answers are complicated and change over time, but we can make some generalizations.

> But what are "values"?

Suppose, for example, that a company asserts that its sole purpose is to maximize profits for its shareholders. Is such an aim among the corporate values that architect Bob Petras has in mind? Probably not. But fortunately, most corporations can develop broader and more significant goals than large dividends. In fact, most corporations *begin* their existence with a powerful set of values. They start out as the embodiment of one person, or of a small group of people, with some strongly held and publicly acknowledged beliefs about the way things *should* be. (" *We felt we were on a mission.*") These beliefs tend to be invoked, explicitly or implicitly, whenever an important decision is made. Over time, they are captured in a series of legends about the company. These legends, told and retold, help establish an organization's moral center and make the company's values accessible to newcomers.

Legends are not always cumulative. Rapid growth, among other things, can break the continuity of oral history. In the late 1960s, Herman Miller's top executives had a series of discussions with management consultant Peter Drucker about this very challenge. During one of those discussions, they described the company's growth in the previous year and projected its growth over the coming year.

In response, Drucker emphasized the need to make Herman Miller's many new employees well aware of what the company was all about and what it was trying to accomplish. "Without this knowledge," he said, "growth will be very difficult." [1]

Herman Miller has taken pains to create and convey knowledge about itself and about its values. Max De Pree, son of Herman Miller's founder D.J. De Pree, calls oral history "tribal storytelling." In his book *Leadership Is An Art,* he makes the case that "history can't be left to fend for itself." Not only has Herman Miller tended to its history, but the company has also translated those values into a language aimed at helping architects. This act of translation has always been difficult and often frustrating. Ultimately, it has resulted in Herman Miller's getting the architecture it needed.

A language aimed at helping architects.

A value: stewardship

In 1980, D.J. De Pree, then 89 years old, talked about the relationship between Herman Miller and its designers. The particular word he chose to describe that relationship was "custodianship."

As De Pree saw it, custodianship carried with it great responsibilities. The person who owned a wonderful work of art and put it in a closet, said De Pree, would not be exercising good custodianship. Turning to an example closer to his West Michigan roots, De Pree described the prosperous farmer who, despite the hunger of countless people in the world, chooses to let his fields lie fallow. That farmer, De Pree concluded, is doing something very wrong.

D.J. De Pree

Many in West Michigan are descended from a group of Dutch settlers who followed the Reverend Albertus van Raalte and other old-country pastors into the area in the mid-nineteenth century. Like New England's Pilgrims, these Dutch settlers came to America as organized churches— whole congregations invoking religious freedom. Perhaps because of this, they built a remarkably cohesive community. Their traditions are still much alive in small cities and towns like Holland and Zeeland.

The traditions of the rural Midwest, despite the gradual extension into the countryside of the Grand Rapids suburbs, also run strong. Good farm land, for example, is treasured. A Herman Miller executive once proposed casually that the company consider building on a 40-acre parcel of property it owned. "Now, that's a perfectly good cornfield," came the stern response. "We had better be sure we know exactly what we're doing before we mess it up."

"Now, that's a perfectly good cornfield . . . ."

It's no wonder, then, that Herman Miller puts a high value on *stewardship*, an article of Dutch-Calvinist faith. The concept meshed seamlessly with the environmental movement in the early 1970s. Nor is it surprising that the company, still rooted in the culture out of which it grew, finds it painful to waste things, to throw things out, to *expend* things—natural resources included. Future generations, too, have a place in the bottom line.

A value: integrity

In the late 1920s, the furniture industry was in deep trouble. It suffered from a crippling lack of originality, reinforced if not caused by an industry-wide absorption with the latest fad. With as many as four new markets a year, inventory was often obsolete even before it could be displayed in the stores. This almost ensured close-outs at deep and damaging discounts.

Store buyers, few of whom understood manufacturing, determined the direction of the market. They dictated terms to the manufacturers: more of this, less of that. In this closed loop, neither the customer nor the manufacturer had much influence. The prevailing furniture styles were heavy and over-ornamented. Moldings, carvings, and other trappings weren't simply an aesthetic preference; they concealed poor workmanship and shoddy materials.

Competition was ferocious; margins were small to non-existent. Surveying this troubled landscape in July 1930, as Herman Miller slid toward bankruptcy, D.J. De Pree reached a painful and surprising conclusion. His industry lacked *integrity*.

At this very juncture, a young furniture designer walked into Herman Miller's Grand Rapids showroom with ideas for a radically different kind of furniture. His name was Gilbert Rohde, and he proposed to create furniture that would draw upon the most appropriate materials for the specific problem at hand. In a sense, it would be "anonymous" furniture, designed to put people first. It would be simple, space-saving, durable—utilitarian. It would reflect, and perhaps even promote, a way of life.

After several spirited discussions, Rohde won his case and was retained on commission. On the strength of D.J.'s faith in this young designer—and also on the strength of De Pree's visit to the 1933 Chicago World's Fair, urged upon him by Rohde—Herman Miller launched the "Modern" furniture business. "Why does this factory concentrate on Modern furniture?" D.J. asked in a 1947 company newsletter. "It is honest in design. Everything looks like what it is. No camouflage as in period design. Woods are used where wood is best and metal where there is structural advantage. The result of this approach is simple functional furniture." A few years later, as the new Eames chairs came onto the market, De Pree could have added molded plastic-polyester to this list. Materials might change, but the concept of integrity did not.

"There's an old Dutch word, *flossy*, which captures all those things that we try to avoid," says Vern Poest, former chief financial officer. "Flossy means all decked out. At Herman Miller, it's not that way."[2]

A value: fairness

The faddishness and volatility of the furniture industry in the 1920s and 1930s contributed to bitter relations between employer and worker. Profits were low and erratic, and so were wages. Layoffs came with little or no warning. In Michigan, whole factories were shutting down and moving south, as their owners sought to escape union wage scales.

For years Herman Miller looked unsuccessfully for ways to break this cycle of distrust and disinvestment. For example: It was extremely difficult to set equitable piecework rates in the factory. Pieceworkers were motivated to compete with each other, rather than to cooperate. Employee suggestions for productivity improvements were rare, and when they were offered, the company found it extremely difficult to put a fair "price tag" on them. Should the worker making the cost-saving suggestion be paid a percentage of the savings? What percentage? For how long: six months? A year? Forever?

At the same time, workers who were paid by the day rates did not have the chance to make bonuses and resented those who did. Profit-sharing, the method adopted by some companies to avoid the evils of piece work, did not seem to make much sense at Herman Miller, since very few line workers could see how their particular work contributed to the company's overall profitability. (Another practical problem at the time: There wasn't much profit to be shared!)

In January 1950 the De Prees read in an issue of *Fortune* magazine an article entitled "Enterprise for Every Man." It told the story of the La Pointe Machine Tool Company, in Hudson, Massachusetts, which had adopted something called the Scanlon plan, an unusual labor/management relations plan, conceived by a cost accountant, turned professional boxer, turned labor organizer named Joe Scanlon. Among other things, Scanlon's plan rewarded workers for making productivity-enhancing suggestions. In the first two years of La Pointe's experience with Scanlon, 350 workers had submitted 518 suggestions and had earned an average of 18 percent in bonuses for those suggestions.

© 1950 Time Inc. All rights reserved

Fortune
January, 1950

The De Prees were intrigued. A month later, they attended a lecture by Dr. Carl Frost, a professor at Michigan State College and a former colleague of Scanlon's. (Hugh De Pree had heard Frost address a group of Grand Rapids businessmen in 1949.) Frost, as it turned out, had helped install the system at La Pointe. In short order, the De Prees invited Frost to do the same for Herman Miller.

To their surprise, Frost resisted. Were they ready, he asked skeptically, to relinquish some of their traditional management prerogatives? Were they prepared to give their employees a great deal of information about the company? Were they themselves ready to work harder?

Only after these questions had been answered to his satisfaction did Frost agree to help. In May 1950 Herman Miller adopted the Scanlon plan. Employee participation and involvement have remained a central tenet of the company's philosophy ever since.

At root, the plan seeks to promote *fairness* in the workplace through participative management. It invites suggestions and awards bonuses, but it goes well beyond that. (Suggestions and bonuses are means, not ends.) The plan seeks to promote cooperation and participation at every level in the organization.

"Everyone who is on the payroll, from the highest to the lowest, has three basic rights: identity, equity, opportunity," said D.J. De Pree in a 1980 interview, citing Colonel L. Urwick, an English author and editor. "Each person has the right to be so identified with the business that he and his family consider it to be *their* factory, on an equitable basis with every other person in the business."

"Everyone . . . has three basic rights: identity, equity, opportunity."

Ownership, in other words, is a key to overcoming anonymity, boredom, and frustration in the workplace. The company's employee stock-ownership plan, established in 1985, carries this philosophy to its logical conclusion.

After a year of service to the company, every Herman Miller employee becomes a stockholder, when the company invests profit-sharing bonuses in company stock.

In the entrance to one of Herman Miller's newer buildings in Zeeland is a dusty machine sporting a much-faded IBM logo. It is one of the time clocks removed from the company's factories in December 1956. Today most employees overlook the relic, mounted waist-high on the wall by some playful colleague. Those few who notice it can reflect on how different their company must have been, four decades earlier, before "identity, equity, and opportunity"—the roots of fairness—came to full bloom.

A value: faith

This brief and incomplete list of Herman Miller's values ends where it started: with faith. In the early years of the company, to most of its workforce, faith would have been understood first to mean a faith in God. In particular, it would have meant the faith practiced by the members of those denominations, principally Dutch Reformed and Baptist, which predominated in the small towns of West Michigan.

Many of the early Herman Miller legends have religious undertones and overtones. Gilbert Rohde's unexpected arrival in the Grand Rapids showroom on that hot July day in 1930 was, to use D.J. De Pree's word, providential. After all, how many companies are saved by a brilliant idea that walks in off the street?

Profound religious faith was not threatened by a sense of humor. "We had lots of jokes about providence," recalls Tom Wolterink, who in his years at Herman Miller supervised the rebuilding of Marigold and the design and construction of Roswell. "If you had a success at Herman Miller, it was providential. If you had a failure, you got chewed out like you would in any other organization."

Over the course of the company's history, faith acquired new connotations. D.J. De Pree's faith in Rohde's unorthodox designs and his willingness to invest in them were amply rewarded. The risky investments made by later generations also paid off, and many times over. Faith and courage had their practical rewards.

From these experiences, the company drew two important lessons. First, it realized that it had to place its faith in the *process* of design. "If there is one thing that distinguishes Herman Miller from most other companies," writes Hugh De Pree, "it is our faith in the efficacy of design. Can there be another American corporation, for example, that has strived with such continuity to help all employees of all levels to understand that the organization's fortunes will rise as high as design will take it?"[3]

Second, the company had to place its faith in *all* employees, not merely in a few top executives. The adoption of the Scanlon plan in the 1950s reflects this kind of faith, though it only formally acknowledged the company's longstanding ideas about the value and potential contributions of each individual.

D.J. De Pree traced this faith in, and respect for, individuals back to an event one morning in 1927. Herman Rummelt, a talented Herman Miller millwright, dropped dead at the factory at the beginning of the first shift. In his role as company president, De Pree visited Rummelt's widow that morning. She talked with De Pree about some of the things that had been most important to her husband. The quality of the many fine, handcrafted objects that adorned the house did not surprise Herman Miller's young president, who was well aware of Rummelt's woodworking skills. Then Mrs. Rummelt read aloud from a number of her husband's poems, which, as it turned out, were equally well crafted. The poems were a surprise to De Pree.

There was another surprise to come, as De Pree later recalled: "Mrs. Rummelt told me about the night watchman we had who was in Rummelt's department. He had been a machine gunner in World War I and had killed a lot of Germans. He thought he was a murderer and was going to Hell. She told me that her husband spent hours between the watchman's rounds sitting with him with the Bible to show him there was reconciliation and forgiveness of sins."

Walking home from Rummelt's funeral, De Pree found himself deeply moved by his experiences at the Rummelt home. They had revealed to him, in a completely unexpected way, the great complexities and hidden strengths of a specific individual within his organization—a person who had come to his attention only as the result of a tragedy.

"I began to realize," De Pree concluded, "that we were either all ordinary, or all extraordinary. And by the time I reached the front porch of our house, I had concluded that we are all extraordinary."[4]

De Pree's intensely personal realization held many implications for the corporation in subsequent years. Herman Miller had to become (as Max De Pree later phrased it) a "place of realized potential." People had to feel free to be extraordinary. The company had to take formal steps, like adopting Scanlon, to identify potential and reward its realization. It had to increase its tolerance for—even encourage—risk-taking and mistake-making. "One factor that made us different," says former chief financial officer Vern Poest, "was the risk-taking, and the rewards that come out of risk-taking. Dutchmen are normally very cautious. They save their

"A place of realized potential."

26

money, they buy their houses, and they never get to Chicago. But here is a small group of people who took an awful lot of risks."[5]

Finally, De Pree's epiphany led to a heightened awareness of hierarchy and power in an organization—and of how their abuse can damage that organization. There are no parking spaces or lunchrooms reserved for executives at Herman Miller. The furniture in the plant rest areas is essentially the same as that in the executive offices. Executive perks are kept to a minimum.

Faith in the design process and in individuals has had profound implications for Herman Miller's products. Like stewardship, integrity, and fairness, faith has had a great impact on Herman Miller's architecture.

Giving guidance through storytelling

Corporate self-understanding (through tribal storytelling) can be an invaluable tool when a company must reach outside itself and engage specialized help. To its outside experts, including its product designers and its architects, Herman Miller *talks* more than it writes, even when written contracts are expected. A short brief, rather than a long one, leaves an architect free to contribute, and leaves the company open to fortuitous discoveries. Trust comes into play. A "faith-full" company has to give people the chance to make mistakes and do their best.

On a number of occasions, Herman Miller has tried to translate its values into written statements about architecture. Six examples follow. Several were written for audiences both inside and outside of the corporation; one was written solely for outside readers. At least three were written with the help of architects. All six have two traits in common: They declare key corporate values, and they attempt to connect those values to architecture.

A "direction statement" (1972)

Herman Miller completed Building E, an 80,000-square-foot addition to the Main Site, in the summer of 1970. By all accounts, it was a spartan facility, designed and built with only minimal architectural guidance. (The company was using much of its capital at that time to produce ever-greater quantities of its successful Action Office furniture.) George Nelson and Gordon Chadwick, the original architects for the complex, were not consulted.

Because Building E was designed as a bare-bones warehouse, Herman Miller made a number of "logical" money-saving decisions. The logic led to poor outcomes. The exterior walls of the addition, for example, were concrete block, rather than the red brick used on the site up to that point. (Logic/received wisdom: *"Warehouses don't need visual appeal."*) Only a thin slab of concrete was poured for the floor. (*"In a warehouse, there is no need for heavy machinery."*) There was little insulation. ("*Energy will always be cheap.*") In a departure from established company tradition, only men's restrooms were installed. (*"Women don't work in warehouses."*) Finally, there were no windows, except at the roof line along the perimeters. (*"Warehouse workers don't worry about seeing outside."*)

"They were not talking about what was best for the employee at that time," recalls one long-time staffer involved in the process. "It was strictly economics."

Max De Pree, returning that fall from a multi-year European assignment, was extremely disappointed with the result and conveyed his disappointment to his older brother Hugh. Herman Miller's chief executive officer in the early 1970s, Hugh responded by asking Max to develop a long-range plan for the Main Site.

Max took on the assignment eagerly. By the following summer, he had hired Los Angeles-based architect A. Quincy Jones to work on a master plan for the Main Site. Shortly afterwards, he established a Building Project Team with five primary purposes: to "review and renew" the long-range plan for the site, to develop a statement of direction, to develop an expansion concept, to facilitate a planned "reunification of office and plant," and to plan future manufacturing and warehouse space.

A. Quincy Jones

In March 1972 the team drafted a "direction statement" for the long-range building program. Drawing somewhat on designer Robert Propst's criteria for the company's newly introduced Action Office system, it read as follows:

This is intended to be a beginning statement of criteria for the next phase of our building program. It is meant to apply to the overall problem of facilities, not just that of a manufacturing plant which, as we all know, can quickly become something else.

It is hoped that these ideas can be the common ground on which we begin the next phase of our building program, but also that we will be open to changing and adding to these thoughts as we go along.

We should try to create an environment that:

Encourages an open community and fortuitous encounter

- Welcomes all
- Is kind to the user
- Changes with grace
- Is person-scaled
- Is subservient to human activity
- Forgives mistakes in planning

- Enables this community (in the sense that an environment can) to continually reach toward its potential

- Is a contribution to the landscape of aesthetic and human value

- Meets the needs we can perceive

- Is open to surprise

- Is comfortable with conflict

- Has flexibility, is non-precious and non-monumental

- In our planning we should know that:

> Our needs will change
> The scale of the operation will change
> Things about us will change
> We will change

It is important that we be prudent stewards of corporate assets, and at the same time we must avoid savings at the cost of good long-range planning and a quality environment.

It is important that we keep future options open. This will demand real discipline, because there is always a great drive to pin everything down if possible.

It is important that we avoid an over-commitment (permanence) to a single function or need. Our own experience has shown us that we need varying utilization patterns open to us and that we need open-ended growth possibilities.

Whatever we do must be constructively involved with the neighborhood and civic community.

It is possible to say that our goal is to build "the indeterminate building."

The key element in being able to achieve our purpose in the planning and implementing of facilities that meet the corporate needs is to influence the value and attitude orientations of all the individuals involved in such a way that they are enabled to be flexible and to participate in the evaluation and the choice of options that are open to us.

"It is possible to say that our goal is to build 'the indeterminate building.'"

A "new building" memo (1975)

Max's De Pree's far-ranging planning process, instigated by Hugh De Pree and masterminded by Quincy Jones beginning in 1971, returned to Hugh in 1975. At that time, Hugh was asked to write down his thoughts about a proposed new Main Site building intended to house executive offices, including his own.

"We are committed to excellence," Hugh wrote of the proposed new space. "This must be translated into our own working and living. We must be perceived as being committed to excellence. . . . Herman Miller has been a leader in the design and cultural change in the last 40 years. Let's reflect that in our offices."

Then De Pree discussed the specifics of his own philosophy and work habits, suggesting how his beliefs and traits might be expressed through architecture:

My philosophy of management is open, rather than closed. Open, because I believe that we will be continually surprised by the performance of people—that given the opportunity, people are usually better than you think they are. People, therefore, need a framework within which they can operate; they should know the rules of the game; they should have enough play so they can fill in their ideas. While they should have help defining the problem, they should be involved enough in it so that they own the problem and become willing and eager to implement the solution.

I can best help them by being an enabler, giving them whatever they need by being a resource to them and by not threatening them unnecessarily when they fail. People must be allowed to make mistakes. . . .

People want to know where I stand. They need direction—they want to know clearly where the company is going, and the role which they play in this direction. . . .

I work best through interactions with others—through a series of short, disciplined sessions—disciplined from the point of view of content and time.

I also think business should be fun—should be enjoyable. If it isn't, then we are not fulfilling all of our personal goals. . . .

I would like to be able to see outside from both the open and closed spaces. . . .

I would like to have access to the outdoors . . . .

I would like to have my office encourage openness and contact with other people—a friendly, warm place, not a countryclub atmosphere— not a living-room in a home atmosphere, but a place where there is performance—where work gets done in a warm and friendly way.

"I would like to have my office encourage openness and contact with other people."

The Bath brief (1975)

The Zeeland master planning effort soon proved to be an invaluable resource on another continent. When Herman Miller began looking for a British architect to design a small manufacturing facility in the United Kingdom—the company's first plant away from Zeeland—Max De Pree laid out his architecture-related thoughts in a short brief for the architects competing for the commission.

The brief reflects an evolution in the company's thinking about architecture. It incorporates some of Hugh De Pree's thoughts: an insistence that the architecture reflect the company's drive for excellence, and the notion that occupants of the proposed building have a sense of relationship to the outside. In spare and precise language, the brief distills the company's values and philosophy into what Nicholas Grimshaw, the architect chosen for the project, later described as poetry:

These statements are intended to structure the program for the planning and building of a new Herman Miller facility for Europe at Bath, England.

Our goal is to make a contribution to the landscape of an aesthetic and human value.

The environment should encourage fortuitous encounter and open community.

The space should be subservient to human activity.

Commitment to performance for single functions or needs is to be avoided.

The facility must be able to change with grace, be flexible, and non-monumental.

Planning of utilities has to meet the needs we can perceive.

We wish to create an environment which will welcome all and be open to surprise.

The quality of the spaces should reflect the company's commitment and reputation in environmental arenas.

Whatever we do must be constructively involved with the neighborhood and civic community.

Utilization patterns should allow for future options for growth and for change.

We would like a building that permits maximum relation of work spaces to the outdoors.

It is possible to say that our aim is to build the indeterminate building.

"We didn't present a written brief to anybody until we did it to interview architects in England," Max De Pree later commented. "It wasn't intended to hem the architect in, but rather, to give the architect a sense of what was really possible. We weren't saying, 'These are the rules we want to live by.' I think we were saying, 'This should give you a sense of the rules that we're *not* going to live by. We don't have a brief for any particular material, for example. You, the architect, solve that—whatever material works.'"

A remarkably durable document, the Bath brief has been used as a touchstone in almost every building project that Herman Miller has undertaken since 1975. It has also evolved. Unique lessons derived from each new building have been assimilated over time and informally worked into subsequent architectural briefs. Gradually, through these various iterations, a relatively clear sense has emerged about "how we at Herman Miller build buildings."

A work team report (1986)

Late in 1985, the company's Facility Management Operations work team tried to capture the various rules of thumb about architecture at Herman Miller. As their starting point, they used the "statement of expectations" created a decade earlier for the Bath plant. That statement's lofty ideals were illustrated by concrete (sometimes earthy) examples:

"The environment should encourage fortuitous encounter and open community."

"The space should be subservient to human activity."

"We would like a building that permits maximum relation of work spaces to the outdoors."

1. *Our goal is to make a contribution to the landscape of an aesthetic and human value.*

   Green areas versus built area for each owned site

   > 25% building
   > 25% roads/parking
   > 50% green

   Provide opportunity for local, regional, and national sculpture on sites.

   Attempt to make our sites part of the community.

   Sites are left open to the community (no fencing).

   No reserved parking space (equity).

   Provide indoor walking space (Spine area in Zeeland) for inclement weather.

   North Fulton Chamber of Commerce used one of the buildings on our Roswell, Georgia site.

2. *The environment should encourage fortuitous encounter and open community.*

   Cafeterias are open to everyone regardless of where they work.

   Spine at Zeeland Main Site.

   Break areas are provided near work spaces in each facility.

The spine at Zeeland

3. *The space should be subservient to human activity.*

   Break areas are provided.

   We are concerned about lighting levels and ventilation.

   Our building standards are higher than the codes regarding building requirements.

   Treat plant areas aesthetically the same as office areas.

4. *Try to develop spaces which support the work functions and desires of employee-owners.*

   Commitment to performance for single functions or needs is to be avoided.

   Construct indeterminate buildings.

   Zeeland Main Site Building B was converted from a manufacturing space to an office facility.

   Grandville Sales Pavilion was converted from factory and warehouse space to an exhibit space.

   The plant office area in the Holland facility is located in a space which was originally designed to be part of the plant.

Green areas versus built area for each owned site:

25% building
25% roads/parking
50% green

5. *The facility must be able to change with grace, be flexible, and non-monumental.*

   When Building B was a manufacturing area, the break area (near large windows and a door) was often mistaken as the "front door." When the building was converted to office space, that area actually became the front door.

   The buildings reflect human scale.

   Utilization of lightweight (people scale) materials.

6. *Planning of utilities has to meet the needs we can perceive.*

   Every location has a master plan prior to the beginning of development.

   Bath, England, has a grid for utilities.

7. *We wish to create an environment which will welcome all and be open to surprise.*

   Sites have no fences.

   Entrances have a sense of arrival.

   There is a sequence of experiences—variety.

"Entrances have a sense of arrival."

8. *The quality of the spaces should reflect the company's commitment and reputation in environmental arenas.*

   Every employee is able to see natural light.

   Burn our own waste to create energy.

   Treat the plant and office spaces the same.

   Energy Center office space allows operator visual contact with space.

   Roswell facility received the IDRC 1982 Award for Distinguished Service in Environmental Planning.

Treat plant areas the same as office areas.

9. *Whatever we do must be constructively involved with the neighborhood and civic community.*

   North Fulton Chamber of Commerce used one of the buildings on our Roswell site.

   Merritt Travel Agency is housed in a corporate facility.

   We have established the standards of quality for buildings in a community when we have moved there.

   Encourage employee participation in civic and neighborhood activities.

   Organized and supported Zeeland Main Street improvements.

10. *Utilization patterns should allow for future options for growth and for change.*

    Each site is master planned.

    Construct indeterminate buildings.

11. *We would like a building that permits maximum relation of work spaces to the outdoors.*

    A view of natural light is available to everyone.

    Provide indoor and outdoor break areas.

    Develop court yards.

    Entrances and exits are quality spaces.

    Green space is provided between parking areas and buildings.

12. *It is possible to say that our aim is to build the indeterminate building.*

    Building B converted from manufacturing space to office space.

    Grandville factory and warehouse space converted to exhibit space.

    Holland plant space utilized for office functions.

A statement of expectations (1989)

In 1989 Tom Pratt, then senior vice president for research, design, and development, concluded that Herman Miller needed a document that would clarify for architects what the company expected from them. A related goal (never far from the company's mind) was to remind Herman Miller people what was important. And finally, the document was intended to help company facilities planners in the pre-programming phase.

Pratt convened a group of nearly two dozen people—architects and designers, as well as most of Herman Miller's senior managers—to talk their way through these issues and ultimately to produce the required document. After several months of intermittent debate, a partial document was produced in draft form. While the pre-programming section of the document was never completed, the following guidelines (based in part on an earlier piece of writing by former Herman Miller board member Bill Caudill, but also an outgrowth of the documents quoted above) served as an effective, more explicit "charge to architects":

Space: In our view, space should not be static and rigid, but, wherever possible, dynamic and fluid, flowing gracefully from inside to outside and outside to inside, allowing freedom of human activity and sensation.

Form: We are not biased toward any one form—plastic, skeletal, or planar. We are interested in the form most suited to a task, context, and economy of means.

Light: We like to build structures that exploit light and its properties to create the best work environment for people.

Structure: We believe that no one structure—whether beam, arch, truss, suspension, or air—*per se,* is better than another. We are concerned only about the pertinence of the structure to the task.

Materials: We are strongly biased toward honest materials used simply, common materials used creatively, materials contributing to a building's value over its useful life.

Connections: We look carefully for superb details, believing as we do that superb details make for superb buildings. We endorse what Charles Eames said about connections: "The connections, the connections, the connections. It will in the end be these details that provide service for the customer and give the product its life."

Proportions: The relation of one element of a building to another and to the whole is very important to us. A building's proportions should spring from the spaces required, the materials, the structure, and the context.

Scale: We want our buildings to be the right scale for their functions ("physical scale"), to fit with human expectations about particular kinds of space ("associative scale"), and to have the power to make people feel comfortable ("psychological scale").

> "We are concerned only about the pertinence of the structure to the task."

Composition: We encourage artistic license on the part of the architect. The architect should deal creatively and to the fullest extent possible with space, form, and light to create the best environment for its type, cost, and function.

Ownership: We will provide various ways for people at Herman Miller to experience a sense of ownership of our buildings and the places where each of us works.

Economy: We want maximum effect with minimum means. We search after elegant simplicity. We want the architect to consider not only initial costs, but also cost/value relationships, cost over useful life, and cost of operation.

Time: Because people and their responses to a building change, we are biased toward buildings that mirror the values, economics, and technology of their time, exhibiting a sustaining character throughout its useful life. If buildings can achieve that quality, we believe they will have long-term value over their lifetimes.

Guidelines for the design of new facilities (1993)

Four years later, the Herman Miller Facilities Group set out to provide even more focused and practical advice to their colleagues who might become involved in building new buildings. With the acquisition of new subsidiaries, some of which had no strong traditions regarding architecture, Herman Miller needed to articulate its core architectural guidelines once again.

In addition to reaffirming the values first laid out in the Bath brief, the new "Guidelines" offered a comprehensive list of specific criteria for new facilities. It also presented practical advice in several new areas, such as financial considerations, perspectives on purchasing land, and approaches to leased facilities.

"How does Herman Miller get buildings to meet these expectations?" the pamphlet asks rhetorically.

By selecting architects who share in our values and who are leaders in ideas, in design, in cost effectiveness, and relevance to the needs of a contemporary organization.

We seek architects who understand that their work will be a commitment to people versus a monument to their talents. In most cases we work with architects who have developed an understanding of Herman Miller. This results in architecture that helps us show our potential as an organization, resulting in an even greater understanding of who we are.

The most important criterion in selecting an architect is our potential to learn from them more about architecture, ourselves, our customers, and about the importance of good design.

"We encourage artistic license on the part of the architect."

"The most important criterion in selecting an architect is our potential to learn from them . . . ."

Conclusion

Legends mount up, and values evolve. A company stuck in its past—especially if it misunderstands that past—will fail to invent its future.

But legends that are cherished and values that are articulated ensure invention. They help lend context and structure to specific and important decisions, both in the short term and the long term.

For example: How can we design the best possible place for our employees? What *is* "best," in the context of this company? According to whom? Why are *those* opinions the important ones?

There is one effective way to put legends to work: by capturing them and expressing them cogently in writing. This explains in part why Herman Miller has taken the time and trouble to generate six architectural "manifestos" in two decades. Aligning buildings and beliefs may be difficult, but it is also a crucial part of enduring architecture.

Who are we? Finding the right answer to this question and getting it down on paper is the best possible foundation for any building.

Marigold

By the mid 1970s, Herman Miller needed a better training and conference center than they could find in the Grand Rapids metropolitan area. A local college had been deeded a 7.5-acre estate on Lake Macatawa's Superior Point, and was having difficulty maintaining the property. The estate, a fifteen-minute drive from Herman Miller's main site, was designed and built at the turn of the century by Talmadge and Watson, and included a 12-bedroom "summer house," a carriage house, a boathouse, and other outbuildings.

In 1977 Herman Miller leased the estate and retained architect William Thrall, of Steenwych-Thrall, to restore and renovate the property. Thrall died early in the renovation process and was succeeded on the job by Chicago-based Nagle, Hartray & Associates, Ltd.

"Our intent," according to an internal memo, "has been to upgrade the land and buildings to a campus setting for our educational purposes and to provide housing for program participants and other corporate guests. The purpose of utilizing this site is to provide a unique experience in an environment which allows a more complete statement about Herman Miller."[6]

New construction was limited to a modest Learning Center (with five meeting rooms and a reception area) and period replacement structures for the decayed boathouse and carriage house. Great care went into a faithful restoration of the lodge—much of it performed by retired Herman Miller employees—and also into the delicate process of winning approval and cooperation from residential neighbors.

The Learning Center at Marigold

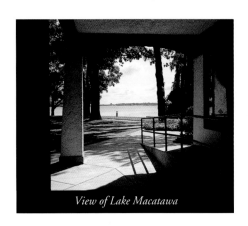

View of Lake Macatawa

Marigold Lodge

Boathouse interior

The Boathouse at Marigold

Embossed on Gordon Nagelkirk's Herman Miller business card, in small gold letters, are the words "40 years." Nagelkirk, former construction manager for the company, is giving several visitors a tour of the Main Site. He is trying to find an example of what he calls "Chadwick Block."

Specified by Gordon Chadwick, who in the late 1950s and early 1960s (along with his partner George Nelson) designed the Main Site, Chadwick Block is a pattern of standard red bricks nested between standard cinderblocks. The 2-inch by 4-inch ends of the bricks, interspersed among the grey concrete blocks, once livened up the building's otherwise drab walls. But because the exterior of the building was entirely clad in brick in 1966, and because most of the original interior walls at the Main Site have long since been knocked down, painted over, or otherwise concealed, genuine Chadwick Block is hard to find.

Finally, on an inspiration, Nagelkirk leads his guests into the southeastern corner of Building B (originally a manufacturing facility and now office space), past some bemused coworkers, and up to an unmarked door. The door opens into a small, dark supply closet, no more than three feet deep. Nagelkirk peers in, squints, turns on a light, and squints again. Then he steps back. With an enthusiastic sweep of a long arm, he points to the back wall of the closet. No real surprise: The wall consists of brand-new looking bricks nested between concrete blocks. "That," he says, smiling, "is just about the best example of Chadwick Block that you're likely to find around here."

For more than four decades, Gordon Nagelkirk was formally or informally responsible for maintaining Herman Miller's West Michigan facilities. When someone in Zeeland wanted to figure out why something was the way it was, they called Nagelkirk.

In the context of a building project, a company is likely to call upon a broad range of outside experts: planners, architects, engineers, project managers, and so on. Before those specialists become involved, though, Herman Miller identifies and involves its internal experts. Some of these internal experts have acquired their expertise by virtue of specialized training or through exposure to a variety of corporate positions. Others, like Gord Nagelkirk, are experts because of their long experience with the company.

All are important. All become teachers to the corporation. The curriculum varies from teacher to teacher, but all sorts of knowledge are required for any organization to keep itself up-to-date, functional, and humane. To put up a building requires a specialized kind of knowledge and experience.

To put up a building that contributes to the life and spirit of a company and a community for years to come requires a certain something else.

So who can teach us? Almost anybody. At Herman Miller, teaching and learning, architecture and architects, human relationships and corporate necessities seem to have become inextricably bound together in the process of building buildings.

Learning from the inside

Who can help? At least four categories of insiders at Herman Miller help think through the earliest stages of a proposed building process. Beginning with the people closest to the action, they are:

Functional and operations specialists

These are the Gord Nagelkirks: the undisputed authorities in their own domains. A domain can be as small as a single key piece of machinery, or it may encompass multiple functions at many sites. If everyone is an expert within 25 square feet of work space (or across 25 buildings), then a company needs to find a way to draw upon that expertise.

Who can clearly state the overriding needs of different functional areas? Who has handled facilities planning in the past? Who best understands the flow of materials and information through the organization? Who has the best handle on the company's transportation needs? Who is best equipped to assess the impact of climate and topography on the proposed facility? Who understands labor forces in different locales? Who can best weigh the operational future of the business?

Honest answers to such questions begin to transform the legends and experience of the company (*Who are we?*) into clear requirements for a new building. They help define what will work and what won't. If we know that we need to be on a railroad line, for example, we know something important about where we *can't* build the factory.

Financial and strategic planners

Why build? Why not lease or buy existing space? Why build now, rather than five years from now?

These are among the questions that confront Herman Miller's financial specialists and strategic planners. As with most questions about allocating resources, the answers require experience, hard work, and good crystal balls. If the company will clearly need to build something eventually, and if

Who can clearly state the overriding needs of different functional areas? Who has handled facilities planning in the past?

construction costs are now climbing rapidly and the rate of inflation is high, can we afford not to build now? If we do build, what kinds of things are likely to happen afterwards?

If corporate resources are scarce, is it wise to tie them up in land, bricks, and mortar? How confident are we in our capital planning process? (When was the long-range capital budget last updated?) What do our latest economic forecasts tell us about longer-term demand for our products?

When it comes time to make choices, the company must be in a position to compare apples to apples. How much does it *really* cost to do it the way we're doing it now, versus the proposed new arrangement? Are there creative ways to combine two or more existing activities, so that a new facility will pay for itself more quickly?

How much does it *really* cost to do it the way we're doing it now, versus the proposed new arrangement?

In the mid-1970s, Herman Miller was looking at the real cost of employee training programs. At the same time, it was determining the real cost of educating and entertaining potential clients. (These costs are sometimes difficult to track and allocate.) A thorough analysis showed that if these two activities could be combined at one site, doing so would more than justify a significant investment in that site. This persuaded the company to invest in the rehabilitation of Marigold Lodge.

Real-worlders

A motley, pragmatic group, real-worlders vary from industry to industry, company to company, and even site to site. They may include lawyers, public-relations officers, lobbyists, development experts, and a whole range of other specialists. These people know how things really *work* out there in the world and how they're likely to be working in the next few years. They study zoning and permitting, local development patterns, the drift of public opinion, and trends in environmental regulations. They can spot government money that might be available (in the form of loans or grants) for specific purposes and are aware of the kinds of strings attached to that money.

Not until Herman Miller figured out the complexities of the federal Economic Development Corporation (EDC) loan program did the company's major expansion program in the 1970s and 1980s became possible. This happened in part because the company had recently hired real-worlder Tom Wolterink, who, with his experience in commercial real estate development in Oregon, encouraged the company to apply for low-cost EDC funding for its proposed facilities.

MARIANNE JEWELL MEMORIAL LIBRARY
BAKER COLLEGE OF MUSKEGON
MUSKEGON, MICHIGAN 49442

The board

Boards of directors differ. Each locates itself somewhere on a wide spectrum, from lethargic to meddlesome. Even the most hands-off board, though, can contribute something to the earliest stages of a building process.

For one thing, each board member has a particular perspective on the real world. Most board members have a finger on the pulse of the national (or international) economy. Directors may even have relevant experience in thinking through the pros and cons of a proposed building project.

Herman Miller has traditionally had an activist board. The board has given early guidance on proposed building projects and also set limits on those projects. It continues to do so—with fitting circumspection. "In keeping with its cautious approach to the national economy," as former Herman Miller President Glenn Walters reported in May 1980, "the Board only authorized that the site work for the Roswell project be started. Depending upon our general business climate, approval of further plans of the construction project will be given as appropriate."[1]

Since the 1970s, the company has tried to ensure that at least one person informed about and sensitive to architectural issues sits on its board. Architect Bill Caudill set a high standard in this role. Some of his personal rules-of-thumb have long since been absorbed into company lore. Before Caudill accepted the invitation to join Herman Miller's board in 1972, he insisted on spending some time on his own in Zeeland, Michigan, the small community that hosts Herman Miller's corporate headquarters. Over coffee one morning with a group of local residents, he discussed Herman Miller's reputation. He wandered through the cemeteries, hoping that he would not find plastic flowers there. (He did not.) Only after such eccentric research did he accept the company's invitation. Over time, he taught Herman Miller something about learning.

Bill Caudill

Summary: learning from the inside

Few of the types of people described above know how to design or build a building, but each may contribute to the early stages of planning for one. They are all resources. They need to be identified early, so that their wisdom and skills can be built into the building process.

Taken together, the design and construction processes are a long, long exercise in investigation, information-gathering, consensus-building, and compromise. Creating a good building is an exercise in constant refinement, a continual striving for clarity. What moves this process? Which kinds of compromises are healthy, and which are unhealthy? Where do we think we're trying to go, and what do we know about how we might be able to get there? Who can teach us?

When a corporation begins to think about putting up a new building, it has the chance to learn a great deal. It may learn how little it knows about itself. It may discover how poorly or how well it treats its employees. It may find out that its attitudes toward the community are not what they should be. As with all kinds of learning, much depends on the teacher.

To summarize: The striving for clarity and the deepening of knowledge do not begin when the outside experts arrive. The pace only quickens.

Learning from the outside

In architecture, the formal processes of investigation, information gathering, and analysis that lead to a design are called "programming." Depending on how it is structured, programming may be a clearly separated from the design process. More often, though, it merges imperceptibly into the later phases of the project.

Many companies with extensive experience in building buildings do their own programming and then hand the resulting program to an architect. Others hire consulting firms that specialize in programming. Still others hire an architect who takes responsibility for programming. In these latter approaches, programmers tend to be the first outside teachers.

Programming consultants

A company without extensive experience in facilities design may choose to hire a firm that specializes in programming to run this phase of a building project. Even this decision must be made carefully, though, since the architect who ultimately designs the building will depend on the thoroughness and accuracy of the program. (In fact, this is one reason why most architects prefer to do their own programming.) If the company and its programmers fail to connect, the project may ultimately come up short.

This happened to Herman Miller. The company planned to modify an existing facility occupied by a subsidiary, but the project had only a provisional approval from the board. It seemed premature to hire an architect for a project still in limbo. "We hired a programming firm to help one of our people—call him Joe—figure out what he needed in terms of an expansion," recalls John Stivers, director of major projects for Herman Miller. "What we wanted was to have a really good program to take to the board."

The programming consultants learned a lot about Herman Miller in a short period of time. Then they met with Joe. "They began by asking him

When a corporation begins to think about putting up a new building, it has the chance to learn a great deal. It may learn how little it knows about itself.

45

how he wanted the philosophy of his subsidiary to come out in this expanded facility," Stivers recalls with a wry grin. "Then they asked another philosophical question, and then another, and then another. After about 30 minutes of this, this guy stood up and said, 'I don't need all of this bullshit. I need 100,000 square feet by Christmas.' He kicked us out, the consultants packed up and left, and we wound up hiring a developer to give Joe his 100,000 square feet by Christmas."

Because of the internal client's impatience with the programmers, he was never exposed to an architect (a *teacher*) and the building was ultimately the worse for it. The space came out bland, predictable, and anonymous—in no way linked to the strengths of his company.

Design/build companies

Some firms design and build facilities under a single contract, a soup-to-nuts approach that usually includes programming. The architect works for the design/build firm, rather than the client, and may have little or no direct contact with the client. In fact, there may not be an architect on the project, depending on the project's scope and complexity.

Generally speaking, the advantages to a client of the design/build approach are an early commitment, a single point of contact, a lack of confusion, and timely completion. The disadvantages can be significant. Many design/build firms, especially the largest ones, are oriented toward straightforward industrial design. They specialize in mills, refineries, and other facilities primarily aimed at processing raw materials. When *people* and their needs are the main focus of a proposed building, this process orientation can be a definite disadvantage.[2]

One phase of Herman Miller's Grandville project began on a design/build contract. The company decided, soon after construction started, that it couldn't tolerate the arrangement. The contract was not terminated, but an architect was brought in retroactively. At one especially low point in the process, a senior company official was heard to growl, "Herman Miller doesn't build buildings without architects." Design/build felt more like "build," and less like "design."

A senior company official was heard to growl, "Herman Miller doesn't build buildings without architects."

Why hire an architect?

Why doesn't Herman Miller build a building without an architect? There are several reasons.

First, the stakes are high, both in financial and human terms. Whatever you do, the results are likely to be around for a long time. Retrofitting means paying twice for the same building. With a decreasing supply of certain materials and increasing construction costs, it only makes sense to do it right the first time.

But getting a building right the first time is not easy. "People say it's not brain surgery, and that it doesn't take a rocket scientist to build a building," says John Stivers. "And they're right. Building a building is simple. But what non-architects don't know is *how* it's simple. They don't know the logical questions to ask, at which point along the line. Putting it another way, I don't think buildings that are done by brain surgeons or rocket scientists are nearly as good as those that are done by architects."

"Building a building is simple. But what non-architects don't know is *how* it's simple."

Architects have technical skills. Some are also artisans, and a few are even artists. Such attributes are difficult to describe, let alone quantify, but they can have important implications for a building. Jeff Scherer, who worked on the design team for the Bath facility and later served as the architect of the Design Yard, recently wrote,

Great architecture is a school room. We learn therein about physical properties not previously considered or attended to:
The changing nature of light and color
The movement of sound
The presence of silence
The character of natural material
The presence of form
The effect of and response to gravity
The simultaneous awareness of all four dimensions
The movement of air (natural, not mechanical).[3]

Scherer's perspective, not often found inside a corporation, inevitably pushes, stretches, and changes a building project.

Finally, and in the same spirit, Herman Miller believes that a company's strength is derived, at least in part, from a willingness to identify and draw upon talented outsiders. Joe Schwartz, former head of sales and of the Herman Miller Research Corporation, once commented that vertical integration is the eventual enemy of design innovation.[4] In other words, even if the company succeeded in creating an in-house group skilled at planning and designing its buildings, it would probably turn out to be an unproductive constraint. Like almost every other company in a competitive marketplace, Herman Miller constantly has to look outward. Architects have helped it do so. "Architects are teachers," says Max De Pree. "We work with the person who we think can teach us the most."

Selecting an architect

A logical first step in hiring an architect is to figure out who within the company is going to direct the building project. Is it one person? Is it a team? Will the individual or team members stick it out for the duration of the project? (Continuity helps.)

Patience, good people skills, faith, curiosity, loyalty, flexibility, tenacity, empathy, and the ability to lay down the law are all highly desirable characteristics in any team member. For practical reasons, at least one person on a building team should be able to read blueprints—or should be willing to be committed to learning that skill quickly. Team members should understand the company intimately (*Who are we?*) and should be prepared to represent the various functional areas with an interest in the new facility.

As the leader is being identified and the team is being assembled, Herman Miller is as explicit as possible about the attitude that it expects team members to take toward the architect (or, more likely, the architect's team). Herman Miller stresses openness and a willingness to learn. These two qualities are expected in equal measure from architect and client.

Ten good questions

Once the team is identified, Herman Miller asks a number of questions, at least in a preliminary way. The tentative answers are made available to the prospective architects and can be used in the screening and interviewing process:

1. *Who are we?* See Chapter 2.

2. *How much are we able and willing to spend?* The question invites an orders-of-magnitude answer at this early stage of the game. Low seven figures? High eight figures?

3. *Are there strings on the money?* Herman Miller's Bath, England, facility was self-financed, and the glass-reinforced plastic wall panels were not an issue. The Chippenham plant which followed was in part financed through public pension funds, which meant that plastic walls (and an exposed rooftop structural system) were off limits.

4. *How does the project fit into the bigger picture?* Is it the first of a phased series of buildings? Does it complete something that already exists? How does it fit into the five- and ten-year plans?

    How does the project fit into the bigger picture?

5. *Is there a site?* If so, does it have distinctive features, or is it nondescript? Is there an important context, as in the ancient Roman city of Bath, or is it tucked between a railroad and a highway, as at Chippenham?

"One of the things that makes Bath a special place is that there's always this kind of mist, and there's always a strong sun," says Jeff Scherer, who worked with Nick Grimshaw on the Bath facility. "Together, they give a kind of fuzziness to the city. And the way that Bath stone wears, too—none of the edges stay sharp. It's all part of the visual vocabulary."

We will revisit site selection and the uses of a site once selected in Chapter 5.

Bath

6. *Is it a rehab, a retrofit, or a from-the-ground-up?* The Design Yard, for example, was first conceived as a new facility. Then a consensus began to emerge that Herman Miller's designers and engineers might flourish in a rehabbed mill building, perhaps on the river near Grand Rapids. An exploration of the costs of that approach led to yet another reconsideration. "What is coming out," as one senior manager wrote to the head of the project team, "is a desire to go back to the farm campus-type idea, even if we build it from scratch."[5] It was only after this fundamental question was resolved that the architect was finally approached.

7. *Are we making a statement?* Is the company trying to test a theory or expand a technological application? Is it trying to make a grand (or false) statement to the world?

The Grandville facility started out as an experiment with preengineered buildings. Since the middle 1960s, its rapid growth fueled by the invention and sale of systems furniture worldwide, Herman Miller had been interested in experimenting with "building systems." If building interiors could be produced in a modular way, why couldn't building exteriors? (The company was nearly doubling in size each year, and buildings had to be added in a hurry. In this context, a modular building might be a salvation.) The experiment was not successful. As noted, design/build was too much build and too little design. The process restricted the kind of architect who could be involved in the early stages of the project.

Herman Miller has traditionally avoided grandiose, monumental buildings— the architectural equivalent of ornate moldings on furniture banned at the company by Gilbert Rohde in the 1930s. Nevertheless, the Rocklin, California, facility afforded an opportunity to raise the company's profile on the West Coast. As former CEO Dick Ruch puts it, "We felt that as a newcomer to Sacramento, where we had a large site and where there was a lot of potential for growth, there would be value in making some kind of architectural statement. To have something that would clearly identify where we were, and who we were, would have some real value."

8. *Are we in trouble?* Does the company need an architect in a hurry? "One of our projects fell into a state of disrepair," Tom Wolterink recalls, "and we had to let the architect go. So, on a Friday night, I called up another architect we trusted and said, 'Help! I need to get a big building up and

running in less than 12 months!' Not every architect could have helped us out at that point."

9. *What's the facility supposed to do?* Is it being built around one function or process, or is it expected to have multiple uses? Neven Sidor, who worked with Nicholas Grimshaw on the design of the Herman Miller facility at Chippenham, points out that some buildings, such as printing plants, are designed and built specifically to house a particular machine, and are thereby limited. In Herman Miller's experience, though, this degree of specificity (especially in the early stages of a building project) is nearly always a mistake. The company's experience has shown that circumstances change too quickly to permit much certainty about how a building will be used in a decade, or who its tenants might be. Flexibility—indeterminacy, in Herman Miller terminology—is key.

George Nelson

In the fall of 1977, Herman Miller told Quincy Jones that Building B at the Main Site needed extensive alterations to continue in its role as a central manufacturing site. Jones spent the fall and early winter drawing up the necessary plans. In mid-January, four months later, Jones got a very different mandate: Building B was to be converted to office space as quickly as possible. Fortunately, the flexibility of George Nelson's original design permitted such a conversion. Jones proved equally flexible.

10. *Are there vested interests involved?* Will a family member, a designer, a favorite contractor, or some other figure inordinately influence the project?

Following Quincy Jones's death in August of 1979, the Houston-based architectural firm of CRS was hired to complete the Building B conversion. Furthermore, according to an internal memo, George Nelson himself, the original designer of the site, was asked to "audit" the project.[6] Projects in which other people (alive or dead, active or inactive) will exert a powerful influence require a special flexibility on the part of the architect.

Qualities of an architect

Herman Miller almost always picks an architect rather than a building. This priority sounds simple; but it rarely is. In picking an architect, Herman Miller tries to open itself up to a new bundle of talent and experience with each new building. It expects to be led by its architects, not only within the confines of the building project, but more generally in new avenues of learning and discovery.

Which qualities make for the right architect? Some are implied by answers to the preceding questions. If the building includes highly specialized uses, or if the site presents difficult design challenges, an architect with relevant experience would be helpful. If the project has to be completed

Are we in trouble?

Herman Miller almost always picks an architect rather than a building.

quickly, an architectural firm with some extra capacity (or the ability to add it fast) is needed.

Other qualities:

Some companies seek out star architects. The impulse to hire a star is often associated with the desire to make an architectural statement. But, as Bath architect Nicholas Grimshaw warns, "If you go looking for a superstar architect, you tend to get what he gives you." (Ironically, like some other architects who have worked for Herman Miller, Grimshaw is now something of a star himself.)

The impulse to hire a star also may grow out of a desire for a sure thing. It takes courage to go outside conventional channels, especially when it comes to designing a multimillion-dollar facility. "Big corporations will default to the known commodity, the star architect, rather than putting their trust in an unknown commodity," says Design Yard architect Jeff Scherer.

Herman Miller avoids monuments, but it doesn't necessarily avoid stars. It tries to match the scale, the scope, and the opportunities inherent in the project with an appropriate design firm. It tries to keep a reasonable consistency of corporate architectural style, a portfolio of buildings, and also to allow for a variety of expressions. "I think what we're trying to do now," says former CFO Vern Poest, "is to use different architectural approaches within the same value system. In other words, we pick out someone in a given area, and say, 'He's got the same value system we do.'"[7]

But a compatible value system shouldn't translate into a pushover. "In fact," says John Stivers, "what we want is challenge. We want somebody who asks us the right questions, and somebody we can learn the most from."

"We want somebody who asks us the right questions . . . ."

Finding candidates

The easiest approach, of course, is to hire someone you already know and trust. Who did our last building? Who comes highly recommended by our best-informed board member?

When firsthand knowledge isn't available, Herman Miller seeks advice from people in other companies who have recently been through the building process, or from other kinds of design professionals. "The advice you seek," says Max De Pree, "is indispensable. And you should listen for overlaps in the answers. For example, I called up three different friends who knew architecture and asked them whom we should hire for a project in Sacramento. And they all said 'Frank Gehry.' So I took that as a strong clue that we should meet with Mr. Gehry."

If circumstances permit, hire a trusted architect to find an architect. When Herman Miller decided to create a southeastern regional center for its

Rapid Response network, for example, it hired an Illinois-based architect to investigate the architectural resources of Atlanta. The consulting architect narrowed the search to two firms. "We investigated other firms for you, and find Atlanta architects to be a little monument-oriented," the consultant wrote. "Of these two, we think Heery & Heery are the least so."[8]

Narrowing the field

Herman Miller usually writes a brief, or preliminary project description, to narrow the field. The brief describes the basic challenges of the project and asks each candidate to describe how he or she might respond to those challenges.

Having decided to build its manufacturing facility in Bath, Herman Miller used its European contacts to develop a short list of possible architects. Meanwhile, Max De Pree wrote a brief based on the work that he and Quincy Jones had done at the Main Site. "The original purpose of the brief," recalls De Pree, "was to give the people on our short list an idea of who we were, and how we approached the problem."

> The brief describes the basic challenges of the project and asks each candidate to describe how he or she might respond to those challenges.

When the list is down to fewer than a half-dozen firms, each is invited to make a presentation to Herman Miller. These meetings are not necessarily scripted. "I distinctly remember going up to meet with them for the first time," recalls Mack Scogin, who designed the Roswell facility, "and we were all sitting around the table and just talking. We had asked, 'Should we give a presentation about our work?' And they said, 'Well, we don't know if you should do *that*.' I distinctly remember that I broke up the meeting at one point. I asked, 'Are we being interviewed for something?' They all laughed and laughed. They thought it was the funniest thing they had ever heard in their lives. It was confusing, wonderful, and enjoyable."

In such a meeting, whether scripted or unscripted, Herman Miller looks for clues as to what it would be like to work with this group. How are they reacting to the "givens" we have presented? Have they done their home-work? If well briefed, are they still spontaneous? Do they ask good ques-tions? Do they know about our corporate philosophy and style, and is their presentation in keeping with them? Are they emphathetic?

In one off-site interview, Herman Miller's team was first put on helicopters to buzz the proposed site. They were then taken back to the architect's offices, where they found an elaborate champagne breakfast waiting. (Herman Miller does not serve alcohol at work-related functions.) But the tired and hungry Herman Miller representatives weren't offered anything to eat until *after* a two-hour slide show—even though the overloaded, fragrant banquet table sat waiting in the same room.

Other less obvious hints, both of good and bad, can be gleaned from interviews. Says Tom Wolterink, "The first architect on Marigold was Bill Thrall, who came across in our interviews as a warm and gentle person. These were qualities that I knew Marigold needed."

How eager is a particular candidate to work with *you*, as opposed to simply getting the work? Frank Gehry, the architect who designed the Rocklin, California, plant, recalls his side of the interview process: "When I went to that interview, I felt like, *'God!* how do I show these guys that I'm the right guy! Everything they're talking about, I know how to make it work, and I don't think all those other guys do.' I felt so in sync with what Herman Miller was saying. Those other guys would say they were in sync—we all would!—but I knew how to make it work."[9]

How eager is a
particular candidate
to work with *you*,
as opposed to simply
getting the work?

When an architect has this kind of enthusiasm for a prospective client, it tends to shine through. In many cases, it endures long beyond the interview process and may sustain a project when it hits rocky times.

The final step is to visit the sites of an architect's previous work. On site, people from Herman Miller ask lots of questions. Are the users happy? Were the schedule and budget adhered to? Is the building performing as expected? What fixes have been applied to the building? Is there anything special about the architect's use of light, choice or use of materials, or skill in providing special amenities that will be important to the new project? How well did the two teams, client and architect, work together? Were the surprises happy ones by and large? Would the client use this architect again?

"I remember one site visit I made with Max De Pree," says former vice president Tom Pratt. "The finish details on the stuff the architect took us to see were just appalling. Really appalling. Not well executed, not brought to conclusion. And when we got back, Max said to me, 'Tom, that's going to be a toughie. If you hire him, you're going to have to sit on the details.' Well, we did hire him, and we did sit on the details."

Each team member may want to single out one architectural feature for special attention across the several sites to be visited. That feature need not be a complicated one. "Take, for example, designing a door," as D.J. De Pree wrote in 1947. "There first of all must be a practical approach. The door must be easy to open, large enough so that a person doesn't bump his head going through. The feel of the door and the knob must be pleasant. Then there is a spiritual approach that must affect the design. Where does the door lead to? Is it a place of amusement, a bank, or an institution of learning, or a place to meditate and worship, or a cheerful home? All of these features have to do with designing a door, and if given honest consideration and attention will result in a good door."[10]

Some final observations by architect Mack Scogin about what to look for in architects: "You ought to be selecting them on your judgment about their capabilities beyond the technical skills. Meeting schedules, meeting budgets, keeping the building weather-tight—that's easy. You ought to be judging them on their ability to understand your needs, to listen, to dream, and to fantasize about things. You shouldn't give a damn about what they have done for other people. What you should be interested in is what they can do for you. Can they pique your imagination? Can they take your ideas and transform them? If not, they're just technicians."

How to hire an architect

It might seem that this question had already been answered somewhere in the preceding pages. But finding and hiring an architect are different tasks. Once the architect is selected, how is he or she retained?

One simple step that Herman Miller has omitted more than once is the formal awarding of the job: "Congratulations. We choose you to design our building." This omission has resulted in part from the company's historical lack of interest in contracts. Herman Miller believes in both covenantal and contractual relationships. Both are necessary, but the covenant is far more important, especially in dealing with architects, whose contributions are both physical and spiritual. After all (people at Herman Miller might say) how can you *force* people to do their best? Good work, including good architecture, grows more easily out of a commitment than out of a contract.

"I think we worked on a handshake [at Roswell] for a long, long time," recalls Mack Scogin. "It didn't matter to them. The contract was just a technical thing that happened somewhere along the line."

Bob Petras, Scogin's former colleague at Heery & Heery, confirms this recollection. "I guess it was after our first meeting up there," he says, "when we were leaving and they were citing all these things that they wanted us to do, that I said, 'Well—are we selected?' As I recall, no one from Herman Miller was saying, 'You're it.'"

Still, the ceremony of confirmation is helpful. Contracts do serve a purpose; even Herman Miller eventually signs them. What Herman Miller has discovered, though, is that there is no particular science to it. Some contracts are structured on an hourly basis. Others are hourly with a guaranteed maximum fee. Others are fixed fee, and still others are a percentage of the construction costs. What helps, above all, is clarity. If the project is clearly defined, the contract (whenever it is drawn up) is more likely to be realistic. Any surprises will probably be good ones.

The covenant is far more important, especially in dealing with architects, whose contributions are both physical and spiritual. . . . Good work, including good architecture, grows more easily out of a commitment than out of a contract.

Herman Miller works hard to find an architect it can trust. The early phases of a relationship between client and architect are good opportunities to demonstrate trust. A contract can be an instrument for building (and gauging) trust.

Building trust during the hiring phase makes good business sense, according to Bath architect Nick Grimshaw. "Max De Pree gave us his trust and confidence," Grimshaw recalls. "When somebody does that for you, you're practically prepared to lay down your life for them, because that's worth so much to an architect.

"We've got a job like that going on right now, and my biggest problem is to keep my guys from working all day and all night on it, and beating hell out of the profitability of the project. It's a very interesting phenomenon. If a client gives you his trust, it pays him back with interest. It's a very smart thing to do, from an economic standpoint, if you pick the right person in the first place, and if you've got the nerve."

Lessons learned

Putting up a building is a form of learning. The attitude and approach of the teacher make a great deal of difference, as do the attitude and openness of the students.

After a company's internal experts have been identified and brought on board, it's time for the proposed project to begin to venture beyond the castle walls.

Herman Miller has used several approaches to programming: in-house, consultant-generated, or architect-directed. None of these processes is inherently better, but Herman Miller leans toward letting architects generate their own information.

Many buildings are built without architects. Based on some unhappy experiences, Herman Miller has concluded that almost all buildings should be entrusted to architects. If temporary or purpose-specific space is needed, the company leases existing space.

Finding and choosing the right architect takes time and forces a company to venture into territory that is largely unknown. (To the extent that architecture is art, it differs from business.) Information is gathered and analyzed, options are identified and gradually eliminated, architects are listened to and judged, and the right decision becomes more and more obvious.

Finding and choosing the right architect takes time and forces a company to venture into territory that is largely unknown.

55

"It's not just who you hire," advises Max De Pree. "It's how you hire them." This applies to the kind of brief that is prepared, and also to the kind of contract that is drawn up between client and architect. When the *commitment* is right, client and architect can move on to the next crucial task: identifying stakeholders. This is the subject of the next chapter: *What do we owe?*

"It's not just who you hire. It's how you hire them."

Bath

Chippenham

Concurrent with the Marigold restoration, Herman
Miller was engaged in building its first overseas facility,
on the banks of the River Avon in Bath, England.
The Bath facility grew out of the company's increasing
success in selling its Action Office systems in Europe
and its need to create a European headquarters.

The Farrell Grimshaw Partnership designed the facility,
which consisted of approximately 55,000 square
feet of mixed factory and office space. After involved
negotiations with the local government—which sought
to defend the integrity of the ancient city's architectural
traditions—the building was completed in 1978.
In the following year, the Bath plant was honored by
the Royal Institute of British Architects as one of the
most outstanding buildings created in Britain in years.
It also won the prestigious *Financial Times* Award
for Industrial Architecture.

The Avon River and Bath manufacturing facility

Bath, England, manufacturing facility

Chippenham

"It is possible to say that our aim is to build the indeterminate building," wrote Max De Pree in his conclusion to the "Statement of Expectations" provided to the architect of Herman Miller's first facility in the UK. Reflecting Herman Miller's commitment to flexible office systems, as well as the company's rapid growth, "indeterminacy" became a goal in all subsequent Herman Miller buildings.

In 1983, Nicholas Grimshaw designed a second Herman Miller facility in the United Kingdom—this time at Littlefields, Chippenham. The first phase of the Chippenham plant comprised some 75,000 square feet of manufacturing and office space. It drew heavily on the lessons learned at Bath and incorporated new materials and technologies to achieve even greater flexibility and indeterminacy.

Chippenham, England, facility

Entrance to the Chippenham facility

Many companies ask their financial people the question at the end of a building process: What do we owe?

There are more provocative ways to think about debts and obligations. Corporations derive great benefits from their communities, and from the broader society. What should they give back, in return? One good answer to this question is, "a building that improves the community."

If the corporation asks "what do we owe" early enough, well before the design process begins, some of the answers can be surprising. Most have nothing to do with money. Many have led Herman Miller to think about architects, and architecture, in new ways.

To begin with the obvious: Herman Miller owes to its shareholders a wise investment of corporate resources. The company must create *a building that works*. The facility must be in the right place for the task at hand. It must respond to climate and topography. It must allow the work within it to proceed efficiently. Its cost must be justified by its function. It must work well into the future.

Herman Miller owes its employee-owners (as it calls them) a comfortable and humane environment: in other words, *a building that is respectful of its occupants*. The building must give its people a voice. It must be health-promoting, accessible, and egalitarian in its allocation of resources. It must lift the spirits of the people who work there.

Herman Miller aims to create, along with its buildings, longstanding relationships with the communities in which its facilities are located. It owes those communities *a building that is respectful of context*. At Bath, for instance, Herman Miller often seemed to be working with three architects: Nicholas Grimshaw, from the 20th century; and the two John Woods, 18th-century architects of the city's most famous structures. The company pays attention to local history, current culture, nature and the environment, and the inherent significance of the proposed site.

Finally, Herman Miller acknowledges a debt to the greater society— to groups and individuals not directly connected to the company. Herman Miller tries to build facilities that alter their contexts for the better. The company tries (more or less successfully) to secure designs that can age gracefully and may even turn out to be timeless. Through its buildings, Herman Miller takes part in larger dialogues, such as the long-term development of the field of architecture or the evolving relationship between managers and workers engaged in egalitarian capitalism. When it adds to the built environment, the company tries to choose beauty and grace, and not to opt for financial expediency or short-term gain.

Corporations derive great benefits from their communities, and from the broader society. What should they give back, in return?

Porch at the Design Yard

No facility embodies every ideal, but only a building that aspires to them can be *a building that adds value.*

"Adding value": threadbare from overuse, the phrase still captures the spirit in which Herman Miller tries to build its buildings. Luckily, there is an almost infinite variety of ways for a building to add value to a site and the surrounding community.

A building that works

Neven Sidor, one of the architects in Nick Grimshaw's London office who worked on Herman Miller's Chippenham facility, argues that only a good client can build a good building. One of the most important of a good client's attributes is an overriding interest in how the building is supposed to work. "The client," says Sidor, "needs to be interested in his building as more than just a financial asset. He needs to be interested in it as a thing that *works*—a thing that is enriched by all of its aspects."

This practical priority is reflected in the master plans of all of Herman Miller's buildings. Frank Gehry's proposal for the Rocklin facility in Sacramento called for a building that would "create an honest, open, and enjoyable working environment which simultaneously promotes production efficiency, ease of maintenance, and employee comfort."[1]

But what, specifically, makes a building work? Herman Miller points to five attributes.

Only a good client can build a good building.

In the right place

A building that isn't in the right place can't work. Site selection, a slightly more specific challenge, is examined at greater length in the next chapter, but an internal HMI memo summarizes the key criteria that the company reviews when considering a location:

Must serve our customers.
Area must provide quality of life.
Quality labor and management availability.
Desirable living area without excessive cost of living.
Political environment is friendly.
Energy availability now and future.
In or near a growing major market.
Adequate logistic services.
Material availability.[2]

A building that ignores or fights its natural surroundings won't work.
It may even self-destruct. Jeff Scherer, who worked with Nick Grimshaw on
the Bath facility in the UK and then returned to practice architecture in the
US, comments:

"The thing you have to remember about England is that it's fairly benign,
in terms of climate. There are things that are done in those benign
climates that can't be done here. If you plot the high-technology buildings
on a graph and overlay climate, there's a pretty interesting relationship.
If you go to Brussels, for example, the building has an endoskeleton. If
you go to England, the technology shifts, and it's an exoskeleton. If you go
to Norway, it gets introverted and detailed on the inside.

"So there are places where there's a very moderate coefficient of expansion,
and a single-glazed building works. But here in the Midwest, where there
can be a temperature shift of 50 degrees in the space of a few hours, a building like that would just rip itself apart."

Ultimately, the climate and topography concern the architect, and he or she
is guided by experience, common sense, local partners (if relevant), and
local building codes. From the outset, though, Herman Miller sees itself as
having a role to play: finding the best opportunity inherent in a given
location, rather than imposing an imported notion on that site. At its
Design Yard, for example, the landscaping mimics the grasses and ecology
of the open prairie, rather than recreating the high-maintenance lawns
of the suburbs.

Allows people to do their work

This is the most obvious imperative of all and the easiest for most corporations to endorse. A building doesn't work if the people in it can't
work. Kermit Campbell, the current CEO of Herman Miller, speaks of
"liberating the human spirit" when talking about the company's mission.
Buildings are a part of that liberation. The goal (as summarized in the
Grandville master plan) is "an integrated facility in which all components
interact. Productivity is encouraged as people understand the whole
process and the importance of their individual tasks."

A building doesn't
work if the people in
it can't work.

Function justifies cost

If a company can't afford the building it's putting up, it had better stop.
But this begs the question: How much money is appropriate to spend?
Herman Miller struggles perennially with this question, most often falling
back on a building's function as a way to set an appropriate budget.
The company's warehouses certainly cost less per square foot than its

showrooms. Herman Miller also tries to strike a balance between cost-cutting (solving today's problems) and investment (creating tomorrow's opportunities). It never defines affordable as "as cheap as possible."

The employee newsletters published by Herman Miller during D.J. De Pree's tenure as head of the company made this point regularly. In one issue, for example, English author, art critic, and reformer John Ruskin was quoted as follows:

It's unwise to pay too much, but it's worse to pay too little. When you pay too much, you lose a little money—that is all. When you pay too little, you sometimes lose everything, because the thing you bought was incapable of doing the thing it was bought to do. The common law of business balance prohibits paying a little and getting a lot—it can't be done. If you deal with the lowest bidder, it is well to add something for the risk you run. And if you do that, you will have enough to pay for something better.[3]

Reality has a way of intruding when it comes to budgeting for a building. Herman Miller sets a fixed-and-lean budget for a building up front, and tries mightily to stick to it. But a budget is only one tool for assessing affordability. A sense of one's obligations—to people, community, and the architectural context—is another.

Flexibility

Before the late 1960s, Herman Miller was primarily a residential furniture company. Since then, it has been primarily an office furniture company. The company did not foresee the swiftness or completeness of the transition, brought about by the runaway success of the Action Office product line, a novel panel system that changed offices for people all over the world.

More than any other experience, the sudden and sweeping change taught the company the importance of flexibility. Herman Miller learned that before a building could be finished, the tenant was likely to change. The lesson was learned at some cost and was not forgotten. In the wake of several expensive retrofittings, Herman Miller began to insist on the flexibility comprised in Max De Pree's broader word "indeterminacy."

"Another aspect of organizing the work place," as the Grandville master plan put it, "is the inevitability of change and the opportunity for growth. It is common to view change and growth in terms of unknown and unforeseeable events creating problems in the future of any business. The Grandville plan incorporates change and growth as the basis for planning future facilities. At Grandville, the organizing structure serves to channel growth in a pattern that will serve future needs of Herman Miller, by allowing for change within the facility and free growth of the building envelope."

This is a pretty good model of architectural flexibility: a building that can change inside and out.

A building that respects its occupants

One day in the 1930s, furniture designer Gilbert Rohde and D.J. De Pree were having a conversation about design.

"You think design is the most interesting thing about a house," Rohde observed.

"Yes, I guess I do," De Pree replied.

"Then you're wrong," Rohde continued. "The most interesting thing about a house is the people who live in that house. And I'm designing for those people."[4]

Rohde was making a case for a new corporate priority. Ultimately, he won his argument, and the company was changed in a fundamental way. Rohde's influence persists in the way Herman Miller designs the products it sells. The new emphasis fit in well with De Pree's personal convictions— "show and pretense reveal some things that are no credit to you," he once remarked—but it also turned out that Rohde was attuned to a previously neglected market.[5] Respect for the customer *was* what the customer wanted.

Years later, when it came time for Herman Miller to build new facilities, the company's buildings were directed toward their "customers"—that is, their occupants. The facilities had to be accessible and health-promoting. In as many ways as possible, they had to give their occupants a voice. They had to speak to their occupants' needs, wants, humanity, and hope.

Accessible—to all people

"It seems to me that there are many situations in life in which the organization is too brutal," architect Alvar Aalto once remarked. "It is the task of the architect to give life a gentler structure."[6]

Until recently, the brutality of organizations often fell especially heavily on people with physical handicaps. Building codes have been rewritten, and laws have been passed on the national level, to correct an inequity of access. In virtually all circumstances, however, mere codes and laws are inadequate. Human judgment must come into play. In making such judgments, Herman Miller tries to err on the side of equity and inclusiveness. Access, in any case, means more than ramps and larger restrooms.

"The most interesting thing about a house is the people who live in that house."

Access, in any case, means more than ramps and larger restrooms.

69

When the interior of the recently completed Holland Seating Plant was being fleshed out in the spring of 1980, the question of storage had to be resolved. The storage rooms were primarily holding tanks for materials related to active projects and secondarily places for testing new ideas. One potential location for them was ideal in every way but one: It was on a mezzanine that could not be made accessible to the handicapped.

Since no handicapped engineers were slated to work in the new plant, a facility manager proposed an interim solution. Use the mezzanine for the fully able, he suggested; "in the event that a handicapped engineer is hired in the future, a similar storage area can be made available [elsewhere] for his/her use."

The response from his superior, John Stivers, was unequivocally in the negative. "Equal but separate does not hold," Stivers scribbled across the bottom of the memo.[7]

"Equal but separate does not hold."

Not all such problems can be dealt with so summarily. When the Design Yard, a project carried out on a lean and fixed budget, was in the design development phase, architect Jeff Scherer raised a series of questions without easy answers: "To what extent are the landscape areas to be accessible to the physically impaired? For example, should only hard-surface areas be accessible? This question is not meant to be exclusionary in nature. We simply need to know if every area of the site should be approachable in a wheelchair. This might include, for example, the edge of the pond."[8]

Herman Miller chose equity, electing to make most of the site accessible. In light of the tight budget, however, other amenities had to be given up. Sacrifices of this kind, by the many for the few, happen only in the corporation that weighs in consistently on the side of accessibility.

Giving people a voice

After completing the Rocklin facility, architect Frank Gehry reflected on the people of Herman Miller and how their desire to get involved influenced his design.

Frank Gehry

"These are very direct people," he commented, "working with their hands and with materials, with a kind of straightforward honesty and directness about them. Which doesn't mean that you talk down to them. In fact, that egged me on to be even more sophisticated. There is a level of sophistication there that you can tap into, and work with, and inspire."[9]

In Herman Miller's buildings, according to the 1978 Bath brief that has guided all of the company's subsequent building projects, space should be "subservient to human activity." The Grandville master plan, which elaborated upon that theme, called for a facility that would "foster a sense of community among the employees, while respecting the dignity and importance of each individual."

"All of the people who work in a building have a standing," former CEO Max De Pree argues, "because they can't avoid looking at that building, and they can't avoid walking into it to make their living. And yet, in most cases, they are given almost no opportunity to contribute to the making of that building. So somebody has to speak for them. I think that's one of the reasons I admired [Main Site architect] Quincy Jones so much. He was there every morning at 6:30, giving people a chance to speak."

Occupants can make a building better. The right building can make for better occupants: in terms of recruitment, productivity, and retention. It can also give them a good reason to come to work every day.

Occupants can make
a building better.

History

"When we did the Bath building," recalls Max De Pree, "Nick Grimshaw gave me a list of things to read before we could start the project. They concerned the history of Bath: the Romans setting up the original baths, the architects who designed the city, and so on.

"He also explained that if we found any archaeologically significant material on the site, we would most likely have to give up and move the project. In the old civilization of the United Kingdom, the past would take precedence."

Happily, no Roman artifacts or imperial ruins surfaced on the banks of the River Avon. The building was completed and was subsequently celebrated in the European press, winning the *Financial Times* Award for Industrial Architecture in 1977. De Pree and others at Herman Miller have since attributed at least some measure of this success to Nick Grimshaw's history lessons. Not surprisingly, when the company settled on the region around Atlanta, Georgia, for a proposed southeastern U.S. facility, they again thought about history and the obligations it imposed.

"I grew up here in Atlanta," says architect Mack Scogin, then with the firm Heery & Heery, "so I knew a lot about the nature of the city, its history, its development, and just the manner of the place. I think that had an attraction for Herman Miller. In fact, there were a lot of people at Heery with that same background.

"The problem arose when Herman Miller told us that they wanted a community that had a certain history to it, that had a time element connected to it. Well, we had a little *war* down here, not too long ago, and our history took a beating."

"Well, we had a little
war down here,
not too long ago, and
our history took
a beating."

Tom Wolterink, who supervised the Roswell job for Herman Miller, found that history (and particularly the legacy of that "little war") changed his

71

opinion about a proposed site. When the small town of Roswell, Georgia, became a strong contender for the new facility, Wolterink emulated Bill Caudill's example and went out to the cemeteries looking for plastic flowers.

"So I'm looking at this particular cemetery," he recalls, "and it looked just *terrible*. It was an absolute mess. It was the worst thing I've ever seen. Was Roswell a terrible town, after all? Well, it turned out that this was a *Union* cemetery. Somebody down there was still fighting the war."

Current culture

The larger cultural context (that is, the needs and opportunities of society in the present) concerns Herman Miller when it fits together a picture of its obligations. The town of Roswell first attracted Herman Miller's attention because of its unusual architectural links to the past, which were in turn the result of a historical twist of fate. On his march of conquest across Georgia, Union General William T. Sherman encountered the tiny town of Roswell, which he agreed not to burn to the ground because Roswell King—founder of the town and a fellow Mason—persuaded him to spare it. As a result, Roswell had history and architecture.

The pond at Roswell

Herman Miller chose the greater Atlanta region for other reasons as well. It was the center of the southeastern market, where Herman Miller had no effective presence. In addition, Herman Miller had committed itself to being part of its communities. ("Whatever we do must be constructively involved with the neighborhood and civic community." [10]) Atlanta had established itself, in the eyes of the company, as a tolerant and progressive community. Members of minority groups had told Herman Miller that Atlanta was the Southeastern city in which they felt most comfortable. Here was a context where Herman Miller could achieve the constructive involvement it sought.

Nature and the environment

Natural resources, like human and financial ones, should be respected and used wisely. Most corporations in the late 20th century have accepted the role of steward and accept responsibilities to both present and future generations. Before Herman Miller plows up a cornfield (for the last time) to pour concrete, it tries to ask the obvious questions: "Are we absolutely sure that building belongs there? Says who, and why?"

Herman Miller is an "energy-conscious company located in an energy-intensive state." [11] Being headquartered in West Michigan during a succession of energy crises has indeed raised the company's energy consciousness and, by extension, its environmental consciousness. But concern for the environment has deep roots.

George Nelson, architect of the Main Site and designer of much of Herman Miller's furniture in the post-World War II decades, was once interviewed by author and radio personality Studs Terkel. Terkel asked Nelson what legacy was being left to posterity by 20th-century humanity.

"I think," Nelson replied bleakly, "large piles of rusty junk." [12]

For many companies, including Herman Miller, Nelson's answer is unacceptable. The company's products are designed to improve the human environment in the office and the home; it would be cynical at best to build those products in ways that knowingly damaged the natural environment.

For the same reasons, it would be counterproductive to build facilities in environmentally unsound ways. The "effect on the landscape and our responsibility in pollution control" are important considerations, the company's managers said in a company direction statement written more than two decades ago. "We share a concern and a responsibility for the quality of the environment in which we and our neighbors live and work." [13]

In 1981, acting on this commitment, the company designed and built an ambitious new energy-recovery system, which generates power through the disposal of waste materials. Herman Miller's current goal is to send nothing to landfills by 1995. "The Energy Center," as one observer wrote in the jargon of the day, "is the latest manifestation of the company's investment in future planning, corroborating Buckminster Fuller's theory that the synergy of technology and human ingenuity can transform and enrich the environment of Spaceship Earth." [14]

Fuller, an important contributor to the company's philosophy about architecture, remarked that "On Spaceship Earth, there are no passengers, only crew." This is another way of putting Herman Miller's determination to be good corporate stewards. The phrase adorns thousands of reusable coffee mugs the company gave to employees, in an effort to reduce the use of styrofoam.

"On Spaceship Earth, there are no passengers, only crew."

The demands of the site

Herman Miller looks beyond the general requirements for a prospective location to focus on that site's special qualities and to consider the obligations that might grow out of them. A building, after all, becomes part of the environment. If the company selects this site (as the company might phrase it), what will it owe?

"Bath is in a valley," says Max De Pree of the company's host city in England. "If you go to the north side, the sunlight makes it look one way; and if you go to the south side, the sunlight makes it look another way.

Before the building was built, we went up to the hills on the south side of Bath and sat there for a couple of hours, looking over the city. And we asked ourselves the real question: Do we want to put a manufacturing plant in this valley? Is that what we want to do to a beautiful place like this?"

"It is the most marvelously complete city," says architect Nick Grimshaw of Bath. "This question of how you might do a completely modern building in a historic city like that was a fascinating one. And I think Herman Miller was a bit nervous about that, because they didn't want to offend the city."

"Do we want to put a manufacturing plant in this valley?"

The same sorts of questions arose when Herman Miller began seriously considering a particular site in the Georgia town of Roswell. Architect Mack Scogin recalls Tom Wolterink telling him that if the building was going to be built on that site, a beautiful old family farm, it had to be done *right*. The historical and natural value of the site had to be respected, and its special qualities preserved as much as possible. "We had worked with a lot of corporations by that point," says Scogin, "and very few of them had ever expressed those kinds of concerns. Few took the time to look beyond the bottom line."

While context creates obligations, respect for a given site does not mean surrender to convention. In Bath, a city built largely of a sand-colored lime-stone, Herman Miller erected a building with plastic walls. And in Roswell, an antebellum town of the American south, the company constructed a low-lying building with aluminum walls. "It would have been absurd, in a project of this size, to imitate the farm buildings down the lane or Roswell's Greek Revival plantation houses," as one architectural journal later phrased it.[15]

The choice of aluminum for the cladding of the Roswell building did raise some concerns. At an open meeting during Roswell's design review process, one member of the city's design review committee asked architect Al Morrison if he didn't think there was going to be a lot of aluminum.

Bath schoolboys

"Ma'am," Morrison replied honestly, "240,000 square feet would be a lot of anything."

The architect's obligation is neither to hide nor to mimic; it is to discover and accommodate what's special about a site. The company's obligation is to endorse that effort and bring it to life.

A building that adds value

Perhaps setting out to add value through a building project sounds like too lofty a goal. Herman Miller looks for ways to bring this goal down to earth. They range from the practical to the inspirational. (It helps to look at value from different perspectives.) Some pay for themselves in obvious and concrete ways; others begin and end as leaps of faith.

Altering a context for the better

Herman Miller tries hard to avoid the false dichotomies, the misleading either-or choices, that seem to present themselves throughout the process of building a new facility. For example: Put up either an inexpensive, conventional building or an expensive unconventional one. Either do nothing to a site, or accept the inevitable harm resulting from the imposition of the built environment on the natural one. "Our goal," said the Bath brief, "is to make a contribution to the landscape of an aesthetic and human value." Herman Miller believes that even the best site can be made better, if one owns up to one's debts and pays them.

Even the best site can be made better, if one owns up to one's debts and pays them.

The Midwest Distribution Center, built in Holland, Michigan, between the fall of 1988 and the summer of 1989, was erected on 53 acres of a 161-acre site. As one of the few remaining undeveloped entrances to Holland, the site was of great interest to city officials. What Herman Miller was to do at the corner of I-196 and 16th Street would largely determine what would follow, good or bad. It was the same at Roswell. "Roswell was a major leaping-out into the hinterlands," observes architect Bob Petras. "The project became the anchor for all future development and set a trend toward quality."

In both cases, the company was well aware of its obligations. "This is our opportunity," as senior facility project manager Vern Clark said of the Midwest Distribution Center at the time, "to do something that says we're a good neighbor, and invites others to do likewise." [16] The building was on a very tight budget, but the site was nevertheless protected. Trees in the way of construction were replanted along the future roadway. As at many Herman Miller sites, a pond was created, both to heighten the beauty of the site and to retain run-off water for fire-fighting. Wildflowers and native grasses were replanted along the drive in the wake of construction.

Being welcoming

Herman Miller "tries to make its offices part of the local community," as one writer has observed. "Sites are left open to the community, without fencing, and there is no reserved parking place." [17] Front doors are clearly identified. Facades at the rear of the building, which often have neighbors, too, aren't cheaper or less well detailed than front facades.

Of course, some buildings (although so far, not Herman Miller's) need fencing. As the company sees it, fences are unnecessary evils. After some debate, the banks of the River Avon alongside the Bath plant were left accessible to the community. Even the Design Yard, in which many of the company's future designs are determined under necessarily secretive circumstances, ended up without fences. The building's architect, Jeff Scherer, simply took pains to build privacy into the building.

Being timeless

"We're captivated by things that we think are new," D.J. De Pree told an interviewer in 1980. "Well, that isn't the way we get timeless things. It's dangerous to always be thinking that we've got to have something new." [18]

Landscaping at the Midwest Distribution Center

Timelessness presupposes, at the very least, a willingness to look forward, beyond the near term. For the forward-looking, the ideal though elusive vantage point is at the intersection of business and architecture. "There's the whole issue of whether you view architecture as a commodity or as part of a continuum," says architect Jeff Scherer. "Part of the problem in business, I think, is that buildings have been defined more by tax codes than by history. Before the tax reform act of a few years back, buildings could be written off in 10 or 15 years. So there wasn't much interest in whether buildings could last longer than that." Even the current 30-year write-off period, he adds, is inadequate to promote longer-term thinking.

Timelessness sounds like a static quality, but of course it is dynamic. It entails improvement over time. Charles Eames, celebrated for his enduring designs, often said that he was more interested in how something would look in ten years than how it looked today. "But that's very hard to do, in architectural practice," Mack Scogin comments. "The buildings that get better over time are the ones that are right for the place they're in, basically. And that's not really a measure of their functionality. For the most part, buildings are quite adaptable, in terms of function. What makes buildings *not* work is when they get dated and lose their presence—their spiritual presence, their physical presence—and stop being respected.

"The great buildings are respected by different generations. How do you accomplish this? The only way is to make a building that is all about the time that it's being built. A building that is all about that particular moment and that particular place. If it comes out of that, it somehow becomes timeless."

> "What makes buildings not work is when they get dated, and lose their presence—their spiritual presence, their physical presence—and stop being respected."

According to Jeff Scherer, it's the *process*—rather than a judgment of timelessness which won't in any event be reached for decades or centuries—that is really important: "Herman Miller never defined 'timelessness' in a really strong way. But there was that search for it. That was the wonderful thing about professing it. It forced the question: how *do* you accomplish timelessness?"

Being part of a larger dialogue

One way is to recall values and ideas that go beyond the pop and the faddish. One such value at Herman Miller is its enduring respect for the authenticity of individuals. Each person is inherently worthy of respect; no one derives worth from a particular job or position.

"I think the concept of industrial democracy came to England with Herman Miller," says Bath architect Nick Grimshaw. "In England, middle management won't usually get involved in the process enough, and top management doesn't know what middle management is doing, let alone what's going on on the shop floor. The idea of the top people in a factory strolling around the shop floor, knowing the people and the processes, came over with Max and Herman Miller. It was really a new way of thinking.

"That was one of the reasons people were so interested in the building. It got the *Financial Times* award, which created a lot of interest, and also meant that the *idea* of the building got written up, as well as the building itself."

Advancing architecture and design

Charles Eames, one of the most innovative designers of the century, used to caution his friends at Herman Miller that they couldn't set out to be innovative.[19] On the face of it, a curious admonition; but Eames was trying to distinguish between *goals* and *results*. (In the same spirit, people at Herman Miller often refer to profit as "the result of doing things right.") Though many of the company's buildings have advanced the fields of architecture and design, innovation was a happy outcome rather than a goal. The company rarely puts up, or puts up with, an exotic building. More often, the innovation takes the form of a daring notion, disguised within an unassuming facade.

The distinction between goals and results

Sometimes, truth be told, the architecture has spoken up for itself and demanded that the company take risks and engender controversies. "Any architecture that is any good is controversial," says Phil Strengholt, now a Herman Miller vice president, who helped on the Roswell project. "If it's boring, it's bad."

"I'll never forget it," says Tom Wolterink about the construction of the facility at Grandville, an unremarkable site and, as a result, a real challenge to architect Larry Booth. "The phone rang the whole time that building was being constructed. People were really nervous about that yellow building, and that bright red door. And Larry just kept saying, 'I don't care if they like it or hate it. I want them to remember it.'"

In the same vein, a company can use its buildings to ask tough questions about, for instance, the high cost of design and construction. "The Design Yard," recalls Max De Pree, "was a risky experiment. The idea was that you didn't have to build monumental architecture in order to get good architecture. Frankly, we were reaching the point where we were getting a little fed up with the high cost of buildings in general."

And finally, a building can be an opportunity for a company and an architect to explore a new possibility together. In the late 1950s, for example, George Nelson and Herman Miller examined the notion of a "showboat showroom." This was to be a barge, built according to the architect's specifications and outfitted with Herman Miller products, which would ply the river trade along the Mississippi, Ohio, and Missouri Rivers. After a fairly intensive investigation, including cost analyses and visits to river towns, the idea was ultimately abandoned.

Another such tide, this one taken, rose at Herman Miller's Rocklin, California, facility, principally designed by Frank Gehry. Gehry asked that his friend and fellow architect, Chicago-based Stanley Tigerman, be allowed to design a part of the Rocklin complex. Gehry and Tigerman, as one architectural journal later put it, were "an oddly matched pair indeed."[20] Herman Miller decided to encourage the experiment, and the synergy that resulted may well encourage other architects with dissimilar styles to find ways to work together. If so, Herman Miller, which owes a lot to architects, has returned a favor.

> "The idea was that you didn't have to build monumental architecture in order to get good architecture."

Lifting the spirit

A last and most important way in which a building can add value is by lifting the human spirit—that is, by providing opportunities for fun, playfulness, and even joy. Easier said than done, especially in the competitive, seemingly dispassionate world of business. "In fact," comments Bill Stumpf, who designed Herman Miller's highly successful Ergon chair, "we've rationalized work to the extent that we've taken all the play out of it."

Herman Miller has not accepted joylessness as an inevitable result of succeeding in business. "People at Herman Miller," says architect Jeff Scherer, "take their work very seriously, but they don't take themselves seriously. Joy and humor are an important part of their culture, because it liberates people to be able to understand and to be receptive to new ideas."[21] The first program for the facility that would become the Design Yard, which Scherer ultimately designed, called for a building that would "inspire us to reach beyond ourselves to risk the future," where "we can only be accused of too high an aspiration."[22]

Mack Scogin cautions that for an architect, to "risk the future" is anything but a simple assignment. "When a Max De Pree says that he wants a manufacturing space where everybody in that space says it lifts their spirits," comments Scogin, "that's a totally subjective goal, and it has to lead to a totally subjective solution. That's the difficult part of architecture. All the other stuff's a snap." Then again, by struggling to turn abstractions like "lifting the spirit" and "timelessness" and "indeterminacy" into reality, Herman Miller has placed corporate architecture among the humanizing elements of its world. The struggle is more than justified by the results.

Accepting leadership's debts

By asking "What do we owe?" we have laid out what might be called the debts of leadership. People lead corporations. In so doing, they can and should accept responsibility for the people within those organizations. Corporations, by extension, can lead communities—but only if they choose to.

Building a building is a rare opportunity for individuals and institutions to exert their leadership in positive ways. Most people associated with Herman Miller would say that this is more than an opportunity, it's an obligation. "I think it goes back," says industrial designer Bill Stumpf, "to some kind of belief within a civilization that things like architecture are important, and are part of civilized life."

Leadership requires an invocation of the corporate conscience. It requires a willingness on the part of its leaders to ask open-ended questions— *What do we owe?*—and grapple with the kinds of answers that emerge from those questions.

The best architects bring philosophical notions about obligations down to earth. They blend form and function in a specific context, on a budget, overcoming thousands of small obstacles on the way to a completed building—which, if all goes well, will live comfortably beyond the period of its design.

"If a building serves its purpose well," observes Nick Grimshaw, "and is liked by the occupants and those who pass by, then it will always have a life of its own."[23]

On a blustery day in December 1961, D.J. De Pree read a short statement at the groundbreaking ceremony for the company's second building at the Main Site. He said that for its workers, Herman Miller sought to provide "fifty weeks of work under wholesome conditions, generous monetary and psychic satisfaction, security through fringe benefits and sound company structure, and personal development and growth."

"If a building serves its purpose well and is liked by the occupants and those who pass by, then it will always have a life of its own."

For the communities in which the company was located, Herman Miller hoped to provide "a proper increase to culture and the economic wealth of the community."[24]

Like beauty and order, architecture grows out of the choices that a company makes, consciously and unconsciously. Architecture is not the ineluctable outcome of mysterious doings. Nowhere is it predetermined that corporate facilities must be uniform and uniformly unspirited, or that business buildings must fall apart in twenty years, or that they must hurt the eye or wound the soul. Constrained resources, a poor location, a rush to get the building completed: These are all ways to avoid asking tough questions (before the fact) or to excuse bad choices (after the fact).

After Herman Miller chooses an architect and asks the questions outlined in this chapter, it faces the same nagging and pragmatic processes of design and construction faced by every other builder: getting from here to there.

Nowhere is it predetermined that corporate facilities must be uniform and uniformly unspirited, or that business buildings must fall apart in twenty years . . . .

Holland Seating Plant

Grandville

Holland Seating Plant

Herman Miller's dramatic rates of growth in the heady days of the late 1970s and early 1980s created the need for new domestic manufacturing space. Increased chair production capacity, in particular, was needed. One option—adding capacity at the Main Site—was eliminated for a number of reasons. Herman Miller wanted to avoid the congestion, impersonality, and anonymity that a huge workforce would create at the Main Site. It was clear, too, that new product lines would eventually require new floor space. The company therefore decided to build on a new site.

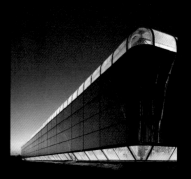

Corner of the Holland Seating Plant

The chair plant in Holland, Michigan—five miles south of the Main Site in Zeeland—was designed in 1979 by a team from Caudill Rowlett Scott Inc., a Houston-based architectural firm led by Paul Kennon and celebrated for innovations in both fast-track construction techniques and facilities management. CRS was also well known for its "squatter team" approach, intended to involve the client in an intensive several-day session of brainstorming with the design team. This approach proved itself in the design of the Holland Seating Plant, completed and occupied in 1980.

Holland, Michigan, site

CRS cofounder William Caudill, who is credited with developing his company's squatter-team approach, helped in the design of the Seating Plant. At that time, he had been serving on Herman Miller's board of directors for seven years —a position he held until his death in 1983. Through his board membership and his writings, he had a profound impact on Herman Miller. "A good building," he once wrote, "properly designed to respond to human needs, helps the learner to learn, the sick to recover, the worker to work, the shopper to shop. Great buildings provide more. They stretch human potential through inspiration."[25]

Production line at Holland Seating Plant

Holland Seating Plant

Grandville

While the Holland Seating Plant was still on the drawing boards in the late 1970s, Herman Miller was also rethinking through a second, partially completed Michigan facility—this one in Grandville, 20 miles northeast of Holland on the then-rural outskirts of Grand Rapids. The company had purchased 22 acres of land in 1977, anticipating the need to create a new facility for its Health/Science Division. This site was eventually expanded to 62 acres.

Initially, Herman Miller intended to use the Grandville site to create an architectural extension of its extremely successful "office systems" products, the now ubiquitous systems furniture that designer Robert Propst invented for Herman Miller in 1968. A company that was almost doubling in size each year had to find an economical and systematic way to build new buildings fast.

This thinking led to a plan for a group of preengineered buildings to be erected on the Grandville site. But when the first two of these buildings were completed, Herman Miller was dissatisfied with the result. Generic buildings, they were neither distinguished nor particularly related to their site. The company then asked architect Laurence Booth of Booth/Hansen & Associates to take over the project and create a combined office-and-manufacturing facility. The new scheme would integrate the two existing buildings with new construction—resulting in a unified structure—and also preserve the option of future expansion.

Booth's design, both aggressive and playful, did not look like the product of a system. Most notable about the building, when completed in 1982, were the colored porcelain panels on its front and side facades: going from white to light yellow to medium yellow , from the ground up. Skeptics called the building "the world's largest Sunoco station," but architect Booth held his ground. "The colors," he explained, "give the building a cheerful and friendly aspect in keeping with Herman Miller's corporate attitude."

The facility has always served as an assembly plant and warehouse. But in the mid-1980s, Herman Miller—needing a new sales and marketing center—turned to Grandville. The New York design firm of Donovan and Green Inc. was asked to create a dramatic space within the building that would showcase (but not overpower) Herman Miller's products. This mandate eventually led to the Herman Miller Pavilion, a dramatic 28,000-square-foot showroom and museum space that played upon and extended the novelty of Booth's building.

Entrance to Grandville, Michigan, facility

Believe it or not, the route from *here* (no building) to *there* (finished build-ing) can be a pretty direct one. The overriding question to be answered, of course, is where is *there?* Where is it that this building is supposed to end up? It's a question highlighted constantly in the preceding chapters, but it also must be asked as we look at the design and construction stages.

This chapter assumes that an architect is on the job, and that good ques-tions (like *What do we owe?*) have been asked and answered.

Recently, in a small town not far from Herman Miller's Main Site, an archi-tect was presenting his latest ideas for a new church building. The design process was fairly far along. But as the building committee listened to the architect's presentation, they became convinced that the there questions had not yet been answered fully. They asked the architect a series of questions:

How are you going to make older people feel welcome here? Have you considered a room with a fireplace, perhaps with special storage for card tables and other equipment nearby?

How are you going to make younger people feel welcome here? Does the church have an opportunity (or perhaps an obligation) to provide spe-cial types of lighting, sound systems, or staging for theatrical events?

How are you going to make the community feel welcome here? Should there be a facility where people from the community, but not necessarily in the congregation, can be married, have receptions, or otherwise mark sig-nificant events? If so, should that be an indoor or outdoor facility, or some combination of both?

What other priorities grow out of the answers to these questions? For example, should there be a full-sized kitchen? A kitchenette? If so, where?

The architect did not have ready answers for these questions. In fact, he confessed, they had not been raised previously. In the relationship between that congregation and its architect, something was going wrong. Was the congregation (or its representatives) not articulate? Was the architect not asking good questions? Was he ignoring their answers?

In Herman Miller's experience, the relationship between architect and client, more than anything else, determines where *there* is. In some cases, "there" may not be a new building at all.

"Sometimes I'm quite surprised," says architect Nick Grimshaw. "People come in and say, 'We want a building.' And I say, 'Well, what do you *do?*' And they say, 'Oh, forget about that; all we need is 20,000 square for so-and-so.'

Where is it that this building is supposed to end up?

The relationship between architect and client, more than anything else, determines where *there* is.

"Well, obviously, I insist on looking at all their buildings, talking to their managers, and understanding their industrial processes before we start anything. And in some cases, I've persuaded them that they don't need a new building. I've shown them that what they ought to do is pull some of their existing buildings down, rationalize the process, introduce a one-way system, or do something else to get themselves straightened out."

In other words, Grimshaw sets out to build a relationship with his client. It is out of this relationship that a building grows—or doesn't grow.

Nicholas Grimshaw

Building the team

In earlier chapters, we looked at how Herman Miller selects its internal team and equips it to think through a building project. In the design and construction phases, a new version of the same challenge arises. Again, a team is built. This time, though, it combines insiders and outsiders. Outsiders include the architect and a number of other skilled professionals.

Who is on the team? The answer depends on the size, scope, and complexity of the project. A good-sized project may include up to a half-dozen people from the client and an equal number from the architect's office. Both "squads" on the team reflect the changing demands of a project over time.

At Roswell, for example, Heery & Heery's squad included Bernard Datsun, who specialized in site selection; Al Morrison, project architect; Bob Petras, head of the firm's industrial project group; and Mack Scogin, Heery's director of design. Datsun completed his work fairly early on, and he was eventually replaced on the team by new contributors.

Herman Miller's squad included five people. Of these, the most important and difficult role was that of project manager, played by John Stivers. "It's difficult for a number of reasons," explains Mack Scogin. "For one thing, you've got a number of technical criteria that you're trying to work towards. But those technical criteria don't always reflect the subjective, spiritual criteria that have been established by the corporation. They're not synonymous. In fact, in 25 years of practice, I don't know if I've ever seen them be complementary.

"But those technical criteria don't always reflect the subjective, spiritual criteria that have been established by the corporation."

"So that position, right there, is one of the most crucial ones. If you've got the wrong person there, with a mediocre, maintenance mentality, you're going to get a mediocre, maintenance-mentality building. If that person's charge is just to keep everybody in line, you're lost. You have no chance at all. If that person isn't smart enough, doesn't have the technical ability, doesn't have the experience, or has no feeling for the goals and objectives of the corporation as a whole, you're lost. You'll never overcome it.

"To me, that's the biggest mistake that organizations make: hiring people in that position who cannot carry on a general discourse on how architecture is made."

Sometimes a project manager represents both the technical criteria and Scogin's "subjective, spiritual" expertise. In other cases, a higher-up in the organization attends, often part-time, to the project's spiritual needs. Tom Wolterink did just that at Roswell (among other places), allowing John Stivers to focus more on the building's technical performance.

Technical issues figure importantly in the composition of the team. The more specialized the facility, the more likely it is that a specialist will join and perhaps remain. Most teams always have room for a Gord Nagelkirk. (See Chapter 3: *Who can teach us?*)

The last question Herman Miller considers while a team is being assembled is, "Who is near the team?" Who is the philosopher, the arbiter of last resort, the voice of principle, who takes ultimate responsibility for the project? Who is the project's champion?

Who is the project's champion?

"I think 'champion' is the wrong word, in Herman Miller's case," remarks architect Jeff Scherer. "I think my word would be 'nurturer,' because 'champion' implies to me the need to elevate and protect. That's not what Max De Pree did for us. What Max did was create an atmosphere where we felt comfortable—a place for us to be vulnerable. They all did that: Max, Tom Pratt, Tom Wolterink, and others. They would challenge the hell out of me in the process, but in the end, they would defer to my judgment. It's a very delicate way to get the best out of somebody, and I think that is what Max is skilled at."

De Pree, for his part, deflects Scherer's compliment. "I wouldn't be persuaded by a book that says that you can only have good architecture if Max is around," he comments. "On the other hand, I don't think you can avoid the fact that somebody has to carry that torch in an informed, compassionate, and hard-boiled way.

"And I'd argue that it has to be the right person. One of the jokes we've had around Herman Miller for years is to say to a salesperson, 'Congratulations; you've really done well; you've reached your sales quota three years in a row; so now we're going to promote you to company pilot.'

"There's a quality of leadership that has to be present. And to put it simply, I'd say that involves being vulnerable to what others bring to the game."

Mack Scogin agrees that there is a difference between the roles of what he calls the "constant presence" and the "constant conscience." Near the team, but not necessarily on it, a diligent conscience has to be lurking:

"You just can't do good architecture without an individual demanding it. That's the only way it's done. A corporation doesn't demand good architecture. Impossible—won't happen! Organizations don't demand excellence. In fact, that's the tightrope that Herman Miller itself has been walking during the last eight or nine years. What happens when that spiritual leadership is lost, or when the baton is not passed on?"

Sites: selecting, acquiring, and redefining

We have already discussed some of the criteria that Herman Miller uses to locate a facility:

Must serve our customers.
Area must provide quality of life.
Availability of qualified employees.
Desirable living area without excessive cost of living.
Political environment is friendly.
Energy availability now and future.
In or near a growing major market.
Adequate logistic services.
Material availability.[1]

In practice, these criteria often boil down to three: proximity to market, community orientation, and aesthetics of the site. In some cases, Herman Miller has identified the site and presented it to the architect; in others, the architect has been closely involved in the site selection process.

The firm that played the most unusual role in site selection for Herman Miller was Atlanta-based Heery & Heery. In fact, Heery went so far as to reject the first site that Herman Miller settled upon. "As we listened to Herman Miller's long-range objectives for future growth," recalls architect Bob Petras, "it became very obvious that the initial site was totally inappropriate. It was on some severe grades, which meant that if you did expand, a tremendous amount of earth work would be needed."

In a peculiar turn of events, Heery then went on to find and purchase a better site for Herman Miller. "I actually negotiated the [Roswell] land deal and bought the property in my name," says Petras. "In fact, I kept it in my name for several months until it was finally disclosed who the buyers were."

Rocklin, California

Herman Miller's Phil Strengholt thinks that the strategy had unexpected benefits. "We were looking for a site," he remembers, "and we kept ending up in tech parks and places like that. So we finally said to Heery, 'Look: here's the money. You know what we think and what we stand for. You find the land that you think will work.' And from then on, all we heard from Heery was, 'Wow! This is a whole new sense of responsibility for us— entrusting us with choosing the site!'"

In selecting the Rocklin, California, site, Herman Miller used a computer model to help make the final determination. "We put quantitative values on a couple dozen criteria, like the price of a home, the quality of life, accessibility to national and state parks, and the cost of living," recalls Tom Wolterink, then vice president for facility management.[2] The quantifiable variables did not obviate judgment. Once again, as in Roswell, Wolterink visited the local cemetery to see how the community felt about its history. He also made a point of talking with teenagers from Rocklin and nearby towns. "They are always an exaggeration of reality," he told a local newspaper reporter.[3]

Tom Wolterink also made a point of talking with teen-agers from Rocklin and nearby towns. "They are always an exaggeration of reality."

Conspicuously downplayed on Herman Miller's list of criteria for a site are tax incentives and other tax-related considerations. "That's because tax laws change over the life of a project," Wolterink explains. "We always felt that when a corporation is induced to go into some area purely because of tax incentives, they'll be sorry in the long run. At best, they'll forget why they moved into that area."

On a parallel track with site selection and purchase is the tangled realm of zoning. Creative site use often necessitates changing the rules, for which changes Herman Miller has always been willing to lobby, provided the community expressed support.

The most dramatic of these changes involved the proposed transformation of Marigold Lodge from a private residence to a planned-unit development (PUD). This involved a significant amount of horse-trading with Marigold's residential neighbors. All wanted the run-down lodge rescued, and most wanted Herman Miller as a neighbor, although with some clear limits. The creative solution eventually settled upon was a limitation on the size of the facility's parking lot. This understanding led to the unanimous support of the neighborhood, which led in turn to the necessary zoning variance.

Roswell, outside of Atlanta, presented a different kind of challenge. There, Herman Miller not only wanted to transform a farm into a factory site, it also wanted to tie the facility's future to the fate of the small city next door. "The promise of a close association with the city, the potential for community identification, and the civic pride in Roswell's history were factors which, when combined with the rural character of the site, provided the impetus for its selection," according to the master plan for the site. "As a condition of purchase, and by request of Herman Miller, the property was annexed into the City of Roswell and rezoned for light industrial use."

A second, more informal condition agreed to by the local community involved access. The town agreed to support the building of a new road adjacent to the site, improving access to the nearby interstate and bypassing the congested center of town.

Sometimes the final approvals don't come until far into the design process. In Bath, the city council postponed final approval for the proposed Herman Miller facility until it could review an architectural model produced by Nick Grimshaw's office. "There was some high-level anxiety," recalls one participant, "about this thing resting there on the side of the Avon."

Picking a track

Most design-and-construction jobs follow one of two tracks. On the more traditional track, the architect designs the building and then bids out the job to one or more contractors. The alternative is fast-tracking, which is just what the name implies: a way to get a building done quickly. Construction of a fast-tracked building usually begins well before the design is fully worked out.

"The Building B conversion project was released one year earlier than was expected," according to the minutes of a 1980 meeting at Herman Miller's Main Site, "and as a result, it will be an extremely fast-track project, and many phases of design, demolition, and construction will be occurring simultaneously. This means we will not be afforded the luxury of a full set of construction documents prior to the commencement of the work."[4]

Some situations seem to call for fast-tracking. One is the undeniable need to finish as soon as possible, as a result of which the client is willing to give up some control (over project budget, project design, or both) to get there. The Building B conversion at Herman Miller's Main Site is an example. Fast-tracking also seems appropriate when construction costs are rising so rapidly—due to general inflation or a high demand for contractors' services—that moving slowly threatens to cost too much.

Herman Miller has used both approaches, to both good and not-so-good effect. The Holland Seating Plant was fast-tracked, mainly because the need for additional chair-manufacturing space was so great. Results were mixed. On one hand, the building was completed on time and even won awards for its user-friendly design. On the other hand, the confusion associated with the fast-tracked nature of the job led to mistakes and shortcomings. (See Chapter 6: *What can go wrong?*)

The Design Yard was also fast-tracked, again because Herman Miller was convinced that the need for the facility was pressing. "I think that project suffered a lot for fast-tracking," recalls architect Jeff Scherer. "I think the quality of the construction suffered, for example. We were fighting mud; we were fighting all kinds of stuff. We had people working night and day. I was flying over there three times a week. My family suffered. Nothing was on an even keel.

"In that case, we should have worked everything out in advance, and then conventionally bid it. I think it would have ended up costing about the same, and there would have been less bloodshed."

Programming

As noted in Chapter 3, the formal investigation, information-gathering, and analysis that lead to the design of a building are collectively known as programming. Most architects argue that because their designs must grow directly out of a building's program, architects should have as much influence as possible on shaping that program. As will become clear in the following paragraphs, programming and designing are almost inextricably intertwined.

"The program is built up in a form of dialogue," explains Nick Grimshaw. "You generate it from an understanding of the client's needs. I think if you don't go to the trouble of understanding those needs really carefully, then you can't get a good building."

Except in dire circumstances, such as the death or unplanned departure of the architect, Herman Miller agrees. Programming is a dialogue, and a vital one. It establishes all of the various performance criteria for the proposed building, ranging from the lofty, spiritual, and subjective to the down-and-dirty, specific, and concrete. What is this building intended to accomplish (lofty)? How is it supposed to *perform* (concrete)?

"The program is built up in a form of dialogue."

Programming is also the stage when important procedural issues are sorted out. For example: How will the team evolve? How will presentations be made? Who will manage the communications flow, including the critical task of note-taking and minute-writing? Who on the client's squad is (or will become) fluent in blueprint reading?

Programming is also a stage, like all others, when team members look ahead into the subsequent stages. What can we say about the overall design and construction schedule (preferably in terms of time-elapsed, rather than tied to specific dates)? What is the budget as of today, and how often will it be reviewed? Will construction be supervised by a general contractor or by a construction manager? Will the job be bid competitively, or will we negotiate a price with a preferred vendor?

Herman Miller has experienced a wide range of approaches to programming, reflecting the styles and preferences of its architects. On one end of the spectrum was Main Site architect Quincy Jones, who specialized in a hands-on, personal style of programming. Here is Jones's account of the process that led to the master plan and program for the Main Site:

"To reach agreement on long-range goals and to move into the planning phase, company representatives and the architect started in 1971 a continuous-interaction chain of communication that continues to this date [December 1974]. Every phase goes through the exchange of input, further study, and more review. Visits to Michigan. Visits to California.

After a brief trip to Michigan in September 1970 and another one early in 1971, the architect introduced the notion of the spine to unify the existing facilities and provide a means for solving the circulation problem . . . .

In November of 1972, he spent two weeks in Zeeland in the factory and worked daily with representatives from each division to obtain detailed information about needs, wants, circulation patterns, movement of materials and people . . . .

Seven additional trips to Zeeland in 1974 gave the architect more opportunities for constructive work sessions in which to exchange information and enrich the quality of the communication, as the drawings and early construction phase proceeded."[5]

During Jones's two-week stay in November 1972, he began every day with a 5:30 a.m. breakfast at a local diner in nearby Holland, where he watched the local routines. Then he went to the plant a half-hour before work started and remained there until well after the work day ended, rubbing shoulders with Herman Miller employees. Operating out of a centrally located conference room, he conducted formal interviews with some three dozen people, and informal sessions with an equal or greater number.

Quincy Jones began every day with a 5:30 a.m. breakfast at a local diner in nearby Holland, where he watched the local routines.

The secret of his approach, as recalled by Elaine K. Sewell Jones, lay in the consistency and flexibility of his questioning. He asked each of his many interviewees the same questions and also left ample room for a spontaneity of exchange. The result was a master plan that had both rigor and intimacy—one which used anecdotal evidence in systematic ways.

More than two decades later, Jones's approach is still remembered and respected at Herman Miller. Much of the specifics of his program have been made moot by subsequent growth and development. But his master plan has had an enduring impact, which even today has subtle but pervasive effects on all the company's activities at the Main Site. For example: the annual company picnic—not an obvious component of master planning!—benefits from Jones' placement of ponds on the site, his decision to include a semi-enclosed courtyard, and his practical locating of bathrooms close to building entrances. For Jones, this part of Herman Miller's calendar was a normal part of the architectural problem.

The obvious success of Jones's Main Site master plan, in fact, has ensured that all subsequent Herman Miller sites have had the benefit of a master plan before any construction began.

One heir to Jones's hands-on, practical tradition is architect Jeff Scherer, who master-planned and programmed the Design Yard in a similar spirit of informal but structured inquiry. "I talked to all those people," he recalls. "I went to the model shop, for example, and talked to all the designers and engineers there. And the first statement that came out was that there could be no windows in the model shop, because they were afraid that [Herman Miller competitor] Steelcase guys would get up on a ladder and look in.

"Well, we worked that through and finally got some windows in the model shop. But I think that sort of participation is a given. It's the way I approach architecture—from the bottom up. Trickle-up architecture."

Larger firms tend to have more formalized programming processes, which have proved applicable across a wide range of clients. Somewhat less formal is Atlanta-based Heery & Heery, which programs in part by means of "predesign product analysis" sessions with the client. In working on the Roswell facility, one predesign product analysis took place in the company of a herd of cows.

"We walked the site," recalls Mack Scogin, "and talked a lot about its various features, and how they might come into play. It was typical of how we conducted those sessions: loosely organized, but with a direction, aimed at achieving certain objectives."

More formal is the "squatter session" approach to programming and design invented by Houston-based CRS co-founder Bill Caudill during intensive programming for two elementary schools in Blackwell, Oklahoma. Two CRS designers spent a solid week with school administrators, students, and parents, and made unexpected progress. Afterwards, Caudill likened their work to squatters, pioneers who squatted on a plot of land until they finally owned it. The name stuck.[6]

The squatter session served Herman Miller well in January 1979, when Tom Wolterink asked for emergency help from Caudill. The challenge: to get a 250,000-square-foot building up and running in less than a year.

"Two days later," Wolterink recalls, "Bill Caudill, [CRS president] Paul Kennon, and three of their top designers showed up in Zeeland, on a snowy night in January. We took them over to Marigold, where we camped out for the next nine days. And the whole seating plant was designed in that time period.

"I'll never forget the squatter-session approach. You take all of these different ideas and put them on 5 by 8 cards, and you paper the walls with facts, goals, and ideas.

"For instance, one of the criteria that came from Max was that everyone should be close to natural light and be able to see the sky and the ground from where they worked. That's because the weather changes so much in Michigan that it's important to know what's going on outside. And it's also just a psychological boost.

"Well, we stood in front of a window at the Learning Center at Marigold and all put X's on the window where our eye-height was. One designer was 6'6", and another was 5'1". So that's where our windows were going to be. And if you look at the Seating Plant, you'll see windows at exactly that height."

One reason the squatter session worked so well for the Holland Seating Plant is that CRS found ways, even under severe time pressure, to elicit existing wisdom about plant design. "We said that we wanted a design," recalls Max De Pree, "that would prevent fork-lift operators from stacking loads against the walls of the building. And that's because we knew that the walls were really part of the lighting system. You can't generate all the light you need just from lighting fixtures; you've got to use reflected light."

Over the past decade, Herman Miller has itself adopted a more formalized approach to programming. The relative looseness of earlier days now seems a bit quaint. "I know that they didn't have in mind exactly what they were going to manufacture here," says Mack Scogin of his experience at Roswell in the early 1980s. "They didn't have any particular, specific goals about how much square footage they wanted, or anything like that. It was more a process of, 'Let's find the right location that will allow us to grow.'"

Within a few years, however, the company's approach to programming was much tighter. A memo on programming, circulated in late 1984, highlights the change: "Just a short reminder and an update of our organization," the memo began. "We are still planning a programming session for your organization's facility needs in early October. To set this session up, I recommend an hour meeting at least a week prior. The meeting should include you, George Cary, Gord Nagelkirk, and me [John Stivers]. . . .

"Experience has taught us that at least four of us in Facilities are needed to run the programming session. Besides me, Gord, and George, an administrative assistant should be involved. Following that point, it will be George and Gord's responsibility to implement the design and construction."[7]

Good arguments can be made for the spontaneity of Roswell. ("We want to be here; now, what do we want?") Still, the increasing willingness of Herman Miller to take responsibility for aspects of programming has led to other kinds of benefits. Being organized earlier in the game enables the company to think sensibly about construction costs during the planning stages. Knowing what percentage fee the construction manager will receive, for example, allows for much more precise budgeting in the programming and design stages. The two stages can, in fact, influence each other in productive ways.

Budgeting for real

Herman Miller has often used the finished program (although programs are never really finished) as a starting point for the budgeting process. In an orders-of-magnitude sense, the program draws upon the expertise of architects and specialized consultants to determine the size and scope of the building, define a rough per-square-foot cost, and create an inventory of the kinds of special technologies and systems needed in the facility. Then the proponent of the project can draw up a proposal to be presented to the board.

Following, for example, is the proposal to Herman Miller's board for the company's new Computer Center:

This is a request for $2,950,000 for a computer center at 8500 Byron Road, Zeeland. The 30,000-square-foot structure, to share the north wall of Building E, includes the computer machine rooms, 17,000 square feet of offices in the computer area, special support equipment for the computer, and a 120-foot extension of the spine and mezzanine. Relocation of the computer operations to this new building will provide adequate space for future growth, minimize the threat of down time due to lack of security or interruption of power, and will allow any terminal at the Main Site to be connected directly to the main frame.

Cost	Description
$ 1,026,444	Building construction
$ 478,222	Mechanical
$ 180,152	Electrical
$ 622,000	Special systems
$ 200,000	Design
$ 175,000	Office systems
$ 2,681,818	Subtotal
$ 268,182	Contingency (10%)
$ 2,950,000	Total

Not all buildings proceed so logically: from program, to budget, to proposal, and only then to intensive design. Companies are organizations full of humans and individual agendas. Things can get backwards.

In planning one Herman Miller building, it was agreed for political reasons that the cost of the proposed new space could not exceed the cost of leased space. (Various departments were competing for limited resources, and extra money for space would have created problems.) An unrealistically low budget was established for the building, leading to short-cuts down the road. Neither the architect nor the company was satisfied with all the compromises that resulted.

Companies are organizations full of humans and individual agendas. Things can get backwards.

At another time, a Herman Miller insider called a low-cost developer of low-cost buildings—"just short of pole barns," as Max De Pree later described that particular style of design and construction—and got a bid for a soup-to-nuts building. In short order, this proposal was presented to the Herman Miller board. Participants at that meeting recall that there was no architect, no vision of the building's scope and capabilities. There was *only* a budget. The project was rejected out of hand.

"Always," says Tom Pratt, "there has been an operational guy somewhere in the game whose job it was to say, 'That's too much money.' But those guys never understood that the upfront costs of a building are only a minor consideration over the life of that building. They never understood the *impact* of architecture on a place or the significance of its longevity."

"... the up front costs of a building are only a minor consideration over the life of that building."

Budget constraints, like other constraints, can be a good thing. When the budget for the boat house and carriage house at Marigold renovations was cut from $1.5 million to $500,000 as a result of a downturn in the economy, the design of the buildings got noticeably better. "The truth of the matter is," John Stivers recalls, "the fact that we had less money took some elements out of the program that they were having a hard time designing. There was supposed to be an enclosed link between the Learning Center and the other two buildings, for example. When the crunch came, that got cut out, and the architects were glad that it did."

It turns out that the bottom line, especially in the realm of architecture, is not easy to draw. "There's a statistical bottom line," explains Mack Scogin, "and there's some other bottom line, too. That's the 'visionary' bottom line, or some such word. It's the bottom line that will take an organization that's in trouble and stabilize it, for example. That's quite a different kind of bottom line."

Mack Scogin

Scogin worked on Herman Miller's award-winning Atlanta showroom, completed in 1989. Showrooms are traditionally high-finish, high per-square-foot cost centers. When a showroom is designed or redesigned, Herman Miller has traditionally braced itself for the day when the architect reveals the financial bottom line.

"I think I surprised them," says Scogin of that showroom experience, "by saying that I felt that you could just *tell* the architect what the budget was. Just tell me from the start what the program is and what the constraints are. Yes, the budget is only part of that definition; and yes, there are certainly some things that you can't pre-budget very effectively. But if you've done it before, if you have a history, you can budget things reasonably. And you can develop your constraints *before* you get stopped at design."

Design: an overview

Most guides to architecture divide design and construction into three, four, or even five discrete phases with names like:

Schematic design, in which the architect responds in a general way to the guidance provided by the program, assigning rough square-foot totals to different functions, suggesting adjacencies and other relationships, etc.

Design development, in which the architect makes most of the decisions generally associated with design, and in which costs become real (and hard choices start to be made)

Construction documents, which translate the agreed-upon design into a roadmap for construction

Bidding, in which the architect helps the client identify and negotiate with a suitable contractor

Construction, in which the building is built, most often under the supervision of the architect and other client representatives

End of construction, which should be cause for celebration, but sometimes isn't. (John Stivers, veteran of many building processes, calls this the phase for "blaming the innocent and recognizing those who were not involved.")

But each phase of architecture blends almost imperceptibly into the next. Fast-tracking only makes *explicit* the fact that everything is happening at once. Concurrentness is also the reality in most conventional approaches to design and construction: A little bit of everything is usually going on most of the time.

Throughout this process, which more than one Herman Miller architect has likened to an editing process, the architect's job is to listen to problems being articulated by the client and to restate the problems in solvable terms. "People tend to think of architects as people who go around forcing their ideas on people," says Nick Grimshaw. "But that's not true. Your job is to act in your client's best interest—to get the best solution for him. It's *not* you doing your own ego trip."

Herman Miller's experience in designing and constructing buildings suggests three rule-of-thumb ways of getting to the best solution.

The first is to *begin with a set of explicit philosophical positions.* They can come from client or architect. Most architects who have worked with Herman Miller cite the company's insistence on indeterminacy, the flexible, changeable building, and on a people-orientation as the two inescapable, mostly non-negotiable ideas brought to the table. Herman Miller appeals to these ideas to keep the architect on target; the architect can invoke them to keep Herman Miller from wavering.

Architects, too, bring strong ideas to the table from their own experiences, from discussions with the client, and finally from knowledge of the site. Jeff Scherer, architect of the Design Yard, had long been fascinated by the one-mile-square grid imposed on the Midwest back in the days of Thomas Jefferson. Scherer's effort to work within (and against) that grid and its legacy of squared-off pastoralism helped give the Design Yard its special charm.

A second, related way to increase a project's chances of success is to *establish a hierarchy of questions.*

"There are *thousands* of decisions that have to be made in the design of a building," explains Nevin Sidor, who helped design Herman Miller's Chippenham facility. "They range from the really crude ones—like, how do you orient this building on this site?—to the really fine ones, like, how is this door threshold going to be sealed against the floor?

"It's simply not possible to answer all of these questions brilliantly. It's only possible to solve a few things brilliantly, and then to get the rest of the things to work. So it's a matter of deciding what the big questions are in any given project."

Sidor also notes, in passing, that the client's intelligence plays a crucial role in setting priorities. Put positively, smart clients set better priorities: "You need a good brain to get around the many facets of a multi-level problem. You need to be able to hold, on a strategic level, all the different aspects of the problem at once, and then decide on your priorities."

Smart clients set better priorities.

A third general rule is to *give the architect running room.* Herman Miller learned this lesson early, in building its first San Francisco showroom in 1958. "We hired Charles Eames and Alexander Girard to go with me and look at the place that D.J. [De Pree] had selected," former CEO Hugh De Pree recalls. "It was an old pepper factory. And Eames and Girard said, 'We don't like it.' The next thing I knew, they were tearing plywood off the windows of this other building they had found, oohing and ahhing, and rhapsodizing about how much they could do with it.

"I said to myself, 'Well, these fellas tend to know what they're talking about. We'd better listen to them.' And when I confronted D.J. with that, he had the same feeling: Let 'em go."

From the designer's end, Bill Stumpf recalls a similar experience when he was asked to lay out an exhibition of a project with Herman Miller at the Walker Arts Center in Minneapolis. "I was shocked by the fact that [director] Mickey Friedman just walked away from a project immediately after it started. Her attitude was, 'Hey, baby—it's *yours.* It's up to you.' There was none of this, 'Here's a brief, here's a list of criteria,' and so on.

And with that kind of autonomy, I think a special kind of chemistry starts to take place. At least it does with me—I work ten times harder."

Jeff Scherer agrees. "People tend to assume that architects and designers punch out mentally when they go home for the night. But they don't. In fact, the design problem consumes you. It's all-consuming. And what autonomy does is to remove the restraints on that consumption. It allows you to feel consumed, and to really possess that problem. It liberates you to be a freer thinker."

To respect autonomy is not to grant license or sign a blank check. (Scherer confesses that he longed for more interaction with Herman Miller during the Design Yard process, a period when the company was simply too distracted by other events to pay enough attention to the project.) Giving an architect running room requires regular meetings, frequent critiques, and a comfortable give-and-take.

"The client's enthusiasm," summarizes Nevin Sidor, "has to be brought to bear on exciting the architect. And once a client has succeeded in that, he needs to pull back and let the architect do his part."

Design: ideas into forms

How do architects do their part? Every architect would answer that question differently. At its heart, though, design embodies the client's perennial goals and objectives in a series of specific criteria, which an architect then translates into reality.

"Sooner or later," says Mack Scogin, "those two things have got to come together. That's the real difficult part of it, and it's why architecture is not an art. You've got to take these subjective objectives—these dreams—and deal with *reality*. You've got to bring the two together, so that you end up with a realistic dream. In other words, it gets built."

"You've got to take these subjective objectives—these dreams—and deal with *reality*."

Jeff Scherer points to an example close to Herman Miller's heart—indeterminacy. "In order for something to be indeterminate," he says, "it has to be disassociated from the program. As soon as those two things are put together, the design *can't* be completely indeterminate. So what you then have is a hierarchy: the things that can be disengaged from the program to become indeterminate, and the things that can't be disengaged.

"What you wind up doing is guarding the idea of indeterminacy, but within practical boundaries. Say you need drain lines. OK, we won't just give you one location; we'll give you eight locations. But we're not going to give you 180 locations."

The good architect thus resolves conflicts and inconsistencies that inevitably arise. Jeff Scherer heard regularly from all of the people soon to be housed together at the Design Yard that they wanted complete freedom of interaction between their various groups. At the same time, he heard, "But of course *I'll* need a wall around *my* office," or "Of course, for security purposes, we can't have any windows in *our* area."

Scherer's response? "I think we're getting paid to question. When there's a disjunction between what they're saying and what they're doing, that's when it's our job to question. It's our responsibility, as provocateurs, to draw people out of those insecurities, to make it OK for them to say what they really think—inconsistent and all—and not feel like they're going to be banged over the head for it."

Architects as provocateurs to the client.

Sometimes architects push their clients by presenting a wide spectrum of possible design approaches and then listening carefully to the responses. In the Design Yard project, Scherer presented rough sketches ranging from a fairly literal representation of a West Michigan farmyard to a typical industrial design. Scherer's minutes of the meeting summarize the discussion: "Mr. Scherer was told that there was no license to be too whimsical or kooky."

"In fact, that was a very useful exercise," Scherer recalls. "Their reaction was, 'We don't want you to go too far in the farmyard metaphor. We would like some of that, but we're afraid that if you go too far, it will be thought of as Disneyland, and not a place of work.' In other words, we succeeded in pinning them down, in finding out what they would be comfortable with."

And of course, clients with experience and a good eye can advance the discussion. To use Scherer's phrase, they can serve as provocateurs to the architect.

Clients as provocateurs to the architect.

"I remember one meeting we had with Max De Pree," says Scherer, "where we showed an early model of the Design Yard, and I had put seven silos along the southeast side. Max just said, 'Great, but there are too many silos.'

"And I said, 'Why?'

"He said, 'Because if you get too many, then you're devaluing the ones that are there.' Which was true, so we edited some of them out."

Design: protecting the non-negotiable

Design is editing; design is give-and-take. And yet, some things shouldn't be open to editing or horse-trading.

In the summer of 1980, project manager John Stivers agreed with the architect that the new windows in Building B, then being converted from manufacturing to office space, did not have to be operable. Shortly thereafter, he received the following memo, the author of which was not of a mind to negotiate:

Since 1975, Herman Miller's policy has been that a portion of all exterior windows shall be operational. We feel this is an excellent policy, which has helped us on many occasions, and will avoid future retrofits . . . . As you know, we have worked hard to keep this policy intact . . . . Operational windows in office spaces is policy, John; it's something you have known for some time and is non-negotiable. Please correct your earlier decisions on Building B immediately.[8]

While most non-negotiables are the client's to establish for architects, the architect can sometimes invoke them for an inconsistent or forgetful client. Frank Gehry, architect of Herman Miller's Rocklin facility, recalls his own effort to protect a non-negotiable. Not surprisingly, given Herman Miller's emphasis on natural light, the subject was once again windows:

"We fought for the skylights, and we got those, although we didn't get the big ones. And we fought for the variety in the windows, so that as people went around looking out, they wouldn't get 'the slot,' but would get a bunch of different pictures."[9]

A final example of a non-negotiable being defended involves the client overruling the client. The issue was fences. Did they make good neighbors or not? One group at Herman Miller told Jeff Scherer that the Design Yard would have to be surrounded by a 12-foot-high fence to guarantee the security of designs-in-the-making. But Herman Miller's whole tradition had been to favor accessibility. "Whatever we do must be constructively involved with the neighborhood and civic community," as the Bath brief phrased it.

"So at one of our meetings in Chicago," says Scherer, "Max finally said, 'Look, we are not putting a fence around this place. We are just *not* going to do it. We'll have to design it with a fenceless fence.'

"And at that point, a lot of things started happening. The internal courtyard, for example, started happening. The layering of the public and private areas, the idea of a walkway creating secondary turf, the idea that you could take visitors through without creating any real problems—the strength of a lot of that stuff came from the fact that we were *not* going to have a fence."

Bidding/negotiating the job

Herman Miller has bid and built its buildings in almost every conceivable way. To meet a tight deadline, Building D at the Main Site, built in 1970, was bid on a cost-plus basis. Herman Miller went ahead with this arrangement (in which the contractor's fee is set as a fixed percentage of the overall construction budget) largely because it had great confidence in Owens-Ames-Kimball Co. (OAK), a Grand Rapids-based contractor that had already done work for Herman Miller. "We were running a real risk of cost overruns if our management was sloppy," as one summary memo put it, "or if the contractor proved to be unreliable. OAK is to be complimented for their integrity in working with us on the project."[10]

By 1976 Herman Miller was bidding different kinds of projects in different ways. All the action was then still at the Main Site, but it was breaking out into several discrete jobs, on discrete schedules. Plans for the "spine" at the Main Site and for offices off the spine were complete, and those were bid on a guaranteed-maximum-price basis. Again, OAK got the job. The rest of the Main Site renovations ($4.6 million out of a total of $6.8 million) were bid provisionally: a cost-plus-fee basis, with a guaranteed maximum price to be established when all construction documents were complete.

Three years later, things were growing more complicated, with substantial construction away from the Main Site being bid for the first time. When the Grandville facility's architect departed in a dispute, taking his bid-related documents with him, John Stivers and his staff quickly pulled together a binder entitled "Bidding Criteria for the Design and Construction of the Rapid Response Warehouse Facility." It specified that design, general construction, and "work to be assigned by contract" (mechanical, electrical, plumbing, and fire protection) would be the contractor's responsibility. Site surveying, topographic and subsoil exploration, foundation design and engineering, and certain other tasks would remain Herman Miller's responsibility.

Subsequent buildings were bid (or negotiated) in a variety of ways. On several of these projects, Herman Miller was fortunate to be teamed up with one of two architectural firms, CRS and Heery & Heery, which had pioneered the field of construction management. Their expertise extended "backward" into bidding and served Herman Miller well. Heery & Heery, knowing that too loose a construction schedule usually leads to inefficiencies, bid the Roswell job on a very tight schedule. Ultimately, that job came in on time and more than $1 million under budget.

Construction

Because construction consumes most of the money assigned to a building project, it attracts a lot of attention. It is in this phase that all of the hard work described in previous chapters should pay off handsomely. To the extent that a building grows out of that hard work (and conforms to the contract documents!), there won't be many unpleasant surprises.

Detail of Rocklin facility

However a project proceeds, two players must work closely and carefully together—the architect and the client's own project manager. The architect retains a fiduciary responsibility to see that the building is built correctly. Both architect and project manager are likely to have been in on the project in its earlier stages. The challenge in the construction phase is to ensure that both can contribute their best through the project's completion.

During the construction of the Rocklin facility, Herman Miller became uneasy about the quality of the finish work. The company's project manager, John Stivers, rode herd on both architect and contractor. "Stivers was the key," recalls Tom Pratt. "Had he not been on that site, that building wouldn't be as good as it is, nor would it have come in under budget. That guy deserves all the credit in the world for making that happen. I gave him cloak and cover, but he made it happen."

Stivers, in turn, gives credit for Rocklin's success to Herman Miller's Greg Chambers, who moved to Rocklin for the duration of the project. "It was Greg," says Stivers, "who kept the quality in the project."

A decade earlier, Stivers had argued for just this kind of on-site, activist project manager. "I feel there is a need," he wrote, "for the owner to maintain a full-time representative at the site, as well as the need for periodic inspections by the architect or his representative." The project manager's job, according to Stivers, would include "running weekly progress meetings, approval of progress payments, coordination of building contractors and equipment suppliers and installers, and scheduling testing activities."[11]

The project manager also explains the progress of the project to colleagues at the company, for whom the construction process can be mysterious. By this point, they may well have invested their best ideas in a process and may have high hopes for the outcome, only to be frustrated by months of silence and seeming inactivity. Newsletters, articles in employee publications, and hand-holding by the project manager all help.

"I wish I could give you accurate, acceptable dates of completion in each phase of work and ideal environmental conditions in and around all construction," project manager George Cary wrote of the Grandville facility in 1979. "Instead, I am at the mercy of the weather, about which I can do nothing except hope, and material shortages and overloaded contractors, for which I can only make threatening phone calls and search for alternative methods to expedite the process. This I assure you I'm doing. The conquests at times seem small. The construction schedule continues to slide, but not to the degree that it could if allowed to."[12]

The contractor may turn out to be the project's best ally. Mack Scogin recalls what happened when initial bids for Herman Miller's Atlanta showroom came in way over budget: "Through negotiating with the contractor, and making judgments about the quality of materials, we came up with a compromise scheme. And the care and love that the contractor later put into the showroom were worth three times what they were finally paid."

The contractor may turn out to be the project's best ally.

Any project can be improved during construction by ideas from all directions. Employees are a key source. Arnie Becksvoort was the first-shift coordinator at the Midwest Distribution Center, which was under construction in the late 1980s. "When I was talking with [project manager] Vern Clark about some needs of the material handlers," Becksvoort recalls, "I noticed the blueprints showed the width of the dock to be the same as the width of the shipping dock in Building E. But the new dock was to be used for both shipping and receiving. It would have been extremely narrow and tight, especially with the forklifts passing back and forth."[13]

Any project can be improved during construction by ideas from all directions.

Unfortunately, Becksvoort made his observation in November of 1988, two months after construction had begun. Nevertheless, a meeting with the architects was called, and the project team found a way to add an additional 18 feet to the shipping side of the dock at a reasonable cost.

Getting there—a summary

According to Jeff Scherer, three things are needed to get from *here* (no building) to *there* (finished building).

The first is an empathetic understanding, on the part of the client, as to what the architect's job is all about. It involves, says Scherer, an understanding of "the processes that are involved for architecture to go from an idea to a reality."

The second is a clear statement of goals, articulated in any number of ways. "It can be written," Scherer says, "or it can be passed on over dinner. It can come from one individual, or a group of individuals—as long as there is the sense that this mantle is being lifted and the truth is being exposed."

And finally, a building project needs honesty. "It's an honesty about the resources that are needed to make things happen," explains Scherer. "It's a realistic budget, a realistic site, a realistic schedule, and a realistic appreciation for the nuts and bolts of making a building."

To Scherer's three-part prescription, we will add an insight from 18th-century essayist and lexicographer Samuel Johnson. Architect Quincy Jones placed it prominently in the front of the Main Site's master plan:

"Nothing will ever be attempted if all possible objections must first be overcome."

Johnson's observation also pertains to the subject matter of the next chapter—*What can go wrong?*

"Nothing will ever be attempted if all possible objections must first be overcome."

"Nothing will ever be attempted if all possible objections must first be overcome."

Roswell

Roswell

In the late 1970s and early 1980s, while the Holland Seating Plant and Grandville were being designed, a third new Herman Miller domestic facility—much farther from the Main Site—was also in the works.

Herman Miller's rapid growth was straining its existing sales and distribution network around the country. This growing network was accommodated entirely in rented facilities. But when the company committed itself to a "rapid response" policy for filling and shipping orders, it had to acquire facilities within an eight-hour truck drive from its major markets. It also felt a growing need for a stronger presence in the Southeast, among other regions.

In 1980, a 135-acre site was selected in Roswell, Georgia, and the Atlanta firm of Heery & Heery was hired to design some 240,000 square feet of warehousing and assembly space— then second only to the Main Site in terms of size and scope of activities. The first phase of the project was completed in late 1981, and manufacturing began in Roswell early in 1982.

Mack Scogin, one of Heery & Heery's architects on the Roswell project, later cofounded the firm of Scogin Elam and Bray, which was hired in 1989 to design a new Herman Miller showroom in Atlanta. The firm transformed a 10,000-square-foot shell in an otherwise anonymous office complex into what Scogin describes proudly as "another world." A dramatic environment in a thoroughly utilitarian setting, the showroom (later relocated to the Roswell facility) recalled the Herman Miller showrooms designed by Charles Eames in the 1950s and 1960s.

Rosewell master plan

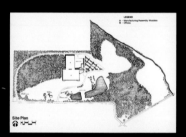

Phase One implementation

Roswell, Georgia, manufacturing facility

The site at Roswell

Outdoor area at Roswell

Entrance area at Roswell

Entrance to Roswell facility

Almost anything.

"All men, no matter how big, make mistakes," D.J. De Pree wrote in 1954. "But history teaches us that big men refuse to falter because of mistakes. Henry Ford forgot to put a reverse gear in his first automobile. Edison once spent over $2 million on an invention which proved of little value.

"The man who makes no mistakes lacks boldness and the spirit of adventure. He is the one who never tries anything new; he is the brake on the wheels of progress. So, don't spend your time regretting mistakes, but get up and hit the line twice as hard. You'll never succeed beyond the mistake to which you are willing to surrender. Remember, a mistake becomes an error only when nothing is done to correct it."[1]

As in most complicated and meaningful processes, the creation of a new workplace includes all kinds of pitfalls. Building a building is a human endeavor disguised as a rational process. In fact, the absence of a few problems in a design and construction process should prompt some questions about the standards that have been set. Have they been ambitious enough?

This chapter begins and ends with mistakes—how Herman Miller tries to think about them, how it tries to react to them, and most important, what it learns from them. For Herman Miller, along with its successes, has had its share of misfortunes.

"All men,
no matter how big,
make mistakes."

Asking bad questions

If you ask bad questions, or don't ask enough questions, or ask them in the wrong way of the wrong people, you'll get bad answers, a problem implied in Chapter 4, *What do we owe?*

The bad question behind one of Herman Miller's buildings went something like this: "To heck with the rest of my disorganized colleagues. How can *my* group get the space it needs as quickly as possible?" Because this bad question went (essentially) unchallenged, the project was ill-conceived and fast-tracked. In other words, the company hit upon a strategy for getting to bad answers by the quickest possible route.

To review the points made in Chapter 4, better questions would have been:

Who am I?

Who is my group?

What do we stand for?

What do we think we need?

Who are my colleagues?

What do they stand for? (Why do they seem so disorganized?)

What do they think they need?

How fixed are these identities, and how urgent are these needs?

How do these identities and needs fit into the bigger context of the corporation?

Who can best answer all these questions?

Had someone remembered to ask the first question above, "Who am I?" Herman Miller might have avoided the ill-fated first draft of one building. The design got all the way to the company's board of directors before it was killed (not without pain). Says Max De Pree, in retrospect, "That solution would never have been proposed if the right person had been asking the questions in the first place."

"That solution would never have been proposed if the right person had been asking the questions in the first place."

A bad question about the cost of another Herman Miller building was, "Can you do it for less than the cost of leased space?" This bad question confused sequence and timing. The question should not have been asked before "it" was defined. (In fact, this was almost the first question the architect heard from Herman Miller.) But it would have been a fair question to ask at the end of the programming stage. At that point, in fact, it would have been a good question.

Getting incomplete answers

It's possible to ask pretty good questions and get bad answers.

One reason might be called the Buffer Syndrome. Designer Bill Stumpf explains: "In the contract furniture system that I'm a part of," he says, "we like to think that we design for the end-user of the product, but in fact, there is a buffer in between. You go into an office building, and a facility manager takes you through and you see these godawful work stations repeated one after another, and you know that this is some facility manager's vision. When you talk with the workers, they'll openly tell you what they don't like about it." Sometimes it's difficult to ask the right question to the right people.

Now transfer Bill Stumpf's dilemma to an architectural context. Good question: "How can we design a building that works?"

Incomplete answer: "Let's make it easier for me to do my job as a facility manager, no matter what." Either the buffer prevents the architect from addressing the right problem, or a good solution is misapplied so that it becomes a bad one. Or worse, an architect mistakes this partial answer for the whole response. Only the client and architect working together can assure complete answers to the right questions.

Breakdowns in relationships

Architecture is all about team-building. The sad truth is that any team may fall apart, especially a team that is at its heart a coalition of people inside and outside an organization, linked only at a point in time for a single project. Even a team of two can founder, whether for important reasons (a debate over a philosophical point) or more trivial ones (a personality clash).

Any team may fall apart, especially a team that is at its heart a coalition . . . .

In a 1981 internal memo, the manager of Herman Miller's computer operations expressed his frustrations over not being heard or heeded in the designing of the company's new Computer Center:

"On both of these points we are at odds with the architects and our own facilities planners. Since *we* must occupy and use the space, and since it will be a very *private* and highly controlled-access area anyway, we feel our requests should be given more weight than they appear to be getting currently from those designing the area."[2]

Although the manager's complaint appears to be directed at CRS, the architects in charge of the project, his real problem was with his colleagues in facilities management. The architect confronted with this kind of internal conflict can do one of three things: 1) Wade in and get clarification (honorable; but difficult, risky, and time-consuming); 2) Stall until things cool off (not honorable, less risky, more time-consuming); or 3) Play divide-and-conquer with the client team (dishonorable, risky, and more time-consuming).

Even Herman Miller, which prides itself on building good relationships with architects, has experienced breakdowns in trust between client and architect. At least one member of the Herman Miller group had a strong sense of what was needed at the Design Yard, and that was a far cry from what Jeff Scherer was inclined (or had resources allocated) to do. "I think we parted ways," says Scherer, "when he made it clear that he was not comfortable with the mental imagery. But I had to keep our commitment to the board, which necessitated a preengineered building. We couldn't do a thing with lots of roof overhangs, lots of brick, and heavy timbers. It just wasn't in the cards, given the budget we had."

There have been other times when the crucial element of personal trust between architect and client evaporated, and circumstances which to Herman Miller had previously appeared innocuous (or even advantageous) now seemed ripe for skullduggery. When the architect asked for permission to bid a proposed building on a "scope of project basis," Herman Miller suspected that fees were being jacked up indirectly. (No doubt the architect would claim that the still-vague project *had* to be bid this way.) The architect's extremely close relations with the contractor on the job, once seen as a lucky coincidence that would lead to good quality control, were

Sometimes the crucial element of personal trust between architect and client evaporates.

now suspect. (Was the architect slipping information to the contractor and thereby causing the contractor's bids to go higher?)

Things came to a head during a dismal planning session at Marigold Lodge. A Herman Miller employee scooped up a set of drawings and announced that the company would use them to get competitive bids on the building. "Oh, no you won't!" the architect shot back. "Those drawings belong to me!" (A correct statement, by the way.) A tug-of-war ensued, perhaps the all-time low point in Herman Miller's relationships with architects.

Bolts from the blue

Design and construction occur where theory and real life converge. Theory has it that things progress in a linear way, from start to finish, with no messy diversions, disasters, or cul-de-sacs. Everybody knows that real life is different, with both fair weather and foul—including what we'll call "bolts from the blue."

Design and construction occur where theory and real life converge.

Saddest case first: The architect dies. This actually happened in the early days of the Marigold renovation, when Bill Thrall suddenly died and had to be replaced by the Chicago-based firm of Nagle, Hartray & Associates, Ltd. Major illness, too, can threaten a project. The lead architect on one Herman Miller building went into treatment for alcoholism. Fortunately, his firm proved more than able to take up the slack.

Even people or problems far from the heart of the project can have a bolt-from-the-blue impact. The Bath, England, plant moved along on schedule until almost the very end of the construction phase. At that point, the supplier of the building's unique, glass-reinforced plastic exterior panels went bankrupt. The result was an unanticipated delay of several months. Similarly, while the Grandville facility was under construction, the US and Canadian employees of Otis Elevator went on strike. The contractor checked with his local elevator specialist and reported with relief to Herman Miller that the subcontractor had all the necessary parts on hand to finish the job. Good planning, or maybe just good luck, avoided a serious delay.

Skewed priorities

Since priorities differ at every company, so do their skewed versions. Two Herman Miller priorities in particular have sometimes come out right, and sometimes skewed: short-term vs. long-term thinking; and determinacy vs. indeterminacy.

The impacts of confused priorities are particularly acute and enduring in the realm of architecture. (You may never really recognize a skewed priority until you build it into a building and live with it—for years, and years, and years.) The unhappy tale of the Main Site's Building E and its subsequent rebuildings has been told in earlier chapters. For Herman Miller, what looked like a bargain first time out soon proved to be an expensive mistake.

Though publicly held companies are always under pressure to deliver good news to their stockholders, architect and board member William Caudill reminded Herman Miller's stockholders at their 1979 meeting that issues of quality, growth, and profits were intimately interconnected. "What costs money," Caudill said, quoting management expert Philip P. Crosby, "are the unquality things—all the actions that involve not doing the job right in the first place."[3]

What looked like a bargain first time out soon proved to be an expensive mistake.

Back to the Computer Center, where confused priorities resulted in a glaring problem. When the facility was first being contemplated, in late 1980 and early 1981, its potential users clearly stated what they wanted. To summarize, the computer people wanted a "windowless block-house," well located, with sufficient technological, security, fire-safety, and expansion capabilities.[4] But neither Herman Miller nor architects CRS could bring themselves to produce a windowless block-house at the heart of the Main Site. (This was too alien, too far removed from all the answers to Chapter 2's central question, *Who are we?*) When the CRS design came back, it specified that the entire east wall of the new facility should be made of glass block.

But what about glare on our screens, asked the computer people? What about the extra heat that will be generated by all that sunlight, requiring extra air-conditioning for our heat-sensitive equipment? Well, came the answer, the window-wall will be made of *reflective* glass block, which will let daylight in but still minimize glare and heat. Reluctantly, the computer people went along, but in the next round of cost-cutting, the reflective glass block was downgraded to ordinary glass block. "It was agreed by those present that the potential for a sun glare problem exists at the exterior glass block wall due to elimination of the reflective block for cost-control purposes," as a CRS memo summarized the meeting. "It was decided that, immediately upon erection of the block wall, CRS and HM, Inc. would make a judgment call as to the need for sun-glaze control devices."[5]

The glass block wall

The Computer Center was built in the spring of 1981 and occupied that summer. By August, it was clear that the glass wall wasn't working. "Direct sunlight on the glass wall creates an intense light inside the Computer Center," as one programmer wrote to his supervisor. "The bright light is an uncomfortable strain on the eyes."[6] Landscaping outside the wall was not having the hoped-for shading effect. Finally, Herman Miller bit the bullet and bought Levelor blinds (five figures' worth) to screen the entire east wall. What went wrong? First, *who we are* was never squared adequately with *what we need.* Second, a short-term cost-cutting measure, one that was recognized in advance as a dubious decision, led to longer-term headaches and expenses. Priorities got skewed.

The other cherished Herman Miller priority of indeterminateness sometimes gets skewed. "It is important that we keep future options open," Max De Pree wrote in 1972, in his introduction to the "direction statement" for the company's long-range building program. "This will demand real discipline, because there is always a great drive to pin everything down, if possible.

"It is important that we avoid an over-commitment to a single function or need. Our own experience has shown us that we need varying utilization patterns open to us, and that we need open-ended growth possibilities."

De Pree and others at Herman Miller were worrying about what they called the "indeterminate building" in 1972 partly because the company had recently completed its Building E at the Main Site, very much a *determinate* building. It could have been transformed from a warehouse to a central shipping area, but no more. "We agree that we want to build a warehouse-type building now because we have a continuing need for warehouse space," wrote one of the sponsors of Building E in 1969, "and we are not planning on using this for manufacturing purposes."[7]

Too determinate—too "pinned down," as Max De Pree might have phrased it—for a company growing by leaps and bounds. The company had to begin to think of itself as a landlord, leasing buildings to tenants within the corporation. Who (in 1969) could predict who a given building's next three tenants might be? In one case at Herman Miller, the tenant changed even before the building was finished.

Overreactions and exuberances

Rounding the last bend before arriving at the Herman Miller facility at Chippenham, England, the cab driver stiffens slightly. "Ugh! Here it comes," she says to her passengers, whom she mistakes for important company officials. "Can't you do something about that *color?*"

Architect Nick Grimshaw worked hard to make the Bath facility fit gracefully into its location in that historic city. The cream-colored, glass-reinforced panels of the exterior walls echoed the tan limestone, the "Bath stone," used for most of the city's buildings. Down the road in Chippenham, however, Grimshaw had a different context: a large, nondescript wedge of land between a busy railroad line and the equally

Who we are was never squared adequately with *what we need.*

"Can't you do something about that *color?*"

124

busy A4 highway. His response was to specify a bright, *bright* blue exterior for the Chippenham warehouse.

"It sits like a space ship in a seemingly alien environment," one generally positive review stated. "[It] gives the impression of having only a temporary association with the site."[8]

To some, including at least one cab driver, bright blue was too much. When it occurs, overreaction is a problem, but it is a problem indicating real human involvement. It implies, at least, that someone has thought hard about something and then reacted.

Architects sometimes overreact to Herman Miller and to its legacy of distinguished design. Frank Gehry, reflecting on another architectural firm's work for Herman Miller, sympathized: "I understand where the mistakes came from. They even came from the very people Herman Miller reveres. The architect's mistakes at that site came from [Charles] Eames. I can just feel it. It was in the air. You get into making Eames-like moves, because you grew up with a reverence for those guys. But Eames works incredibly well with plywood chairs and not so well with buildings."

Some overreactions to an idea become exuberant and run away with themselves. Architects and clients fall victim to this. In the late 1970s, the company became fascinated with the notion of an office building addition at the Main Site to be covered by a "tensile" roof (a double layer of fabric supported by cables under tension). It was, in effect, a plan for a high-tech tent. The company's insurance agents were aghast.

The company's insurance agents were aghast.

"It appears that the fabric will burn through before sprinklers operate," as one of the agents wrote. "This would cause excessive temperatures on the cable supports, and result in structural failure and collapse . . . Even if a suitable material could be found, the roof would have to be designed to normal requirements for windstorm resistance and collapse . . . . These are major problems, which may make it much more attractive to provide a conventional-type structure."[9]

The idea for the Big Top was abandoned. Ideas are powerful. When they become exuberant, they need careful execution, one way or another.

Shortfalls and overshoots

Question: When is a cost overrun not a cost overrun? Answer: When it's the result of an obscure recalculation.

Early in 1980, Herman Miller found itself in a difficult bind. It was fast-tracking a new seating plant in Holland with Houston-based CRS as the architects. The budget for the building was $9.5 million, a figure arrived at through a complex calculation of how much federal Economic Development Corporation (EDC) money was available in the form of loans.

The loans were crucial, since they would save the company at least $6.5 million in interest. As Herman Miller read the law, if the cost of new construction within the relevant municipality (Holland) exceeded $10 million, no EDC money would be available.

Key to the CRS design of the Holland Seating Plant was a "People Place." This was to be a central facility, surrounding the offices and visitors' center and described during the squatter session as "belonging more to the people who work[ed] there than to the visitors."

One day in February or March, someone at Herman Miller sat down, reread the EDC fine print, and discovered something scary. The law actually said that the limit was $10 million *within a ten-mile radius,* not within a single municipality, including manufacturing equipment, which Herman Miller had not counted in its calculations. Herman Miller already had $3 million in EDC-funded capital projects underway within the radius. Suddenly, in a wink, the budget for the Seating Plant had to be reduced by $3 million. The People Place, the heart and soul of the facility, was dead, the victim of a planning shortfall.

Architects, too, make miscalculations, although not usually this dramatic. When the problems of glare and heat at the Computer Center were finally solved, the season changed, and another kind of complaint came in from a disgruntled user:

"We are experiencing major problems with the east entrance into the Computer Center, which need to be addressed quickly. This entrance is a main entrance during the week, and the *only* entrance on weekends when the North Spine door is locked. We use the center 24 hours a day, 7 days a week, with HMI and service people coming and going at all hours.

"Due to its easterly exposure, the snow and ice build up and make this door inoperable. We recently lost over two hours of productive time when an operator could not get into the building on a weekend. The ice and snow also adversely affect the ADT security card reader and intercom phone located there. We have experienced unending problems with this equipment. These doors are also fire exits. On weekends, the ice build-up makes them unusable."[10]

If anything, the problem was understated. The winter of 1981-82 was a particularly snowy one. On some days the snow drifted as high as the building—including on the east wall of the Computer Center. CRS came back to the site and ultimately decided to build a small vestibule to counter the snow and ice-related problems.

If a project is complicated enough, somebody will forget something, and the design will fall short. Quincy Jones, who preceded CRS as principal architect at the Main Site, made a different kind of mistake. According to Herman Miller team members, Jones and his staff tended to overshoot the target. "The thing we experienced with Quincy Jones," recalls Gord Nagelkirk, "was that their engineering staff built everything at 200 percent, rather than 100 percent. For example, after they put the heating equipment on Building F, we found that we only needed two-thirds of it to maintain the heat and air flow in the facility."

The expense was unnecessary, but Herman Miller was eventually able to recover some of it. When Building E was upgraded, the redundant heaters and blowers were stripped off of Building F and moved over to Building E. "But it was," Nagelkirk concludes, "rather an expensive way to go about it."

Bad execution

When it gets right down to it, the general contractor (GC) has to make everything fit together and work. Even in constructing a cookie-cutter housing development, this isn't easy. In a one-off corporate facility, where many things are first-time experiences, contracting can be extremely difficult. Complicating the job is the fact that although the GC is responsible for the quality of subcontractors' and suppliers' work, in most cases he only controls quality through the power of the purse.

"Please be advised that all seven exterior corner skylights have been rejected by HMI, OAK, and CRS," wrote Grand Rapids-based general contractor Owens-Ames-Kimball to one supplier of windows for the Holland Seating Plant. "[We have] tried with maximum effort to install these units. These corners were supposed to be on the job site 12/16/79, but did not arrive until 2/25/80. We feel HM has experienced far too much inconvenience already. These seven new corners MUST be expedited."[11] They were.

And sometimes, the work done on the site simply is not up to snuff. Gord Nagelkirk, steeped in the quality standards of West Michigan, was surprised when he took a trip to a Herman Miller facility in a different part of the country. "For instance," he recalls, "the ceramic tile work there was very irregular. And a few years later, a portion of the floor gave way under some loaded racks in the storage area. We then drilled a number of holes to determine the thickness of the floor, which should have been six inches reinforced with wire. Well, there were places where it was down to two inches, and there were places where it was nineteen inches."

Inconsistencies

This is a client's mistake, common in all sorts of business activities: Vacillate in your position and hold your agent (in this case, your architect) to contradictory standards.

When it gets right down to it, the general contractor has to make everything fit together and work.

Nick Grimshaw rescued Herman Miller from a lapse into determinateness at the Chippenham facility. "Chippenham was really meant to be a warehouse," he recalls. "No mucking about; it was for storage. So it was hard for us to hold on to the idea that anything could happen anywhere. But we *did* hold on to it. And then Herman Miller started saying, 'We don't need so much storage space, but we've got to have somewhere for some more manufacturing. Hey—wait a minute! Didn't Grimshaw say that Chippenham could be turned into manufacturing?' So they took the storage out, put some more glazing in, and it worked extremely well."

Sometimes inconsistencies arise among the members of a project team. At one point, Rocklin's architect, Frank Gehry, began getting mixed signals from Herman Miller.

"I knew," recalls Max De Pree, "that things were not going well with the Rocklin project, and a lot of it was our fault. At one point, I called up Frank and said, 'I'm beginning to get the feeling that it might be helpful if Tom Pratt and I came and talked to you.' Frank agreed. So when we got to his office, he showed us an elevation. He pointed at a particular window and said, 'The engineers say that this window has to be five feet off the floor, because they want to put a machine below it.'

"I blew my stack. That's exactly the kind of instruction you don't give to an architect. The placement of a machine is going to dictate the architect's window scheme? *Really?* How long do we think that particular machine is likely to stay in that particular spot?" Gehry was rescued from a Herman Miller inconsistency, but just barely.

Changing contexts

The Main Site in Zeeland has evolved continuously over its 30-year history, with many architects contributing. Quincy Jones's "spine," a north-south thoroughfare around which the whole facility was eventually supposed to be expanded and reorganized, illustrates the problems that can result from a changing context. After Jones's death, Herman Miller couldn't quite decide what to do with the spine. The company gave contradictory signals to CRS, the architects who succeeded Jones and were charged with finishing a new master plan for the site.

One thing the spine was supposed to accomplish was to tie in an additional 200,000 square feet of manufacturing space at the north end of the site. The utilities had all been laid in the ground; the "trellis" for the northward extension of the spine was in place; and the company needed more manufacturing space. Everything was in place for a significant expansion of the Main Site—but it didn't work out that way. More expansion for increased chair production, farther down the road, would have been difficult; and large numbers of additional workers on the site would have created logistical problems.

With the decision not to expand the Main Site, two things happened: the Holland Seating Plant was born, and the spine lost the centrality that Quincy Jones imagined for it. Today, the spine still runs through the Main Site, and its skeletal extension still juts northward across vacant land to the Energy Center. A victim of changing context, it waits for the time when it can live up completely to its architect's expectations.

Contexts can change in ways which neither client nor architect can anticipate. When Herman Miller located in Roswell, it was a bucolic semi-rural suburb of Atlanta. Today, the once-sleepy town suffers from all of the ills of rapid development: clogged streets, cheap construction, and architectural mongrels. The country town that the Roswell plant was built to be respectful of is, in fact, gone.

Contexts can change in ways which neither client nor architect can anticipate.

Across the ocean, in Bath, a strange reverse image of this problem has arisen. Nick Grimshaw's design for the plant was intended to be *flexible,* above all else. Utilities were more or less moveable. Bathrooms were moveable. And almost every element of the facade was designed to be interchangeable—walls for windows, windows for walls, and so on.

In Great Britain, buildings are "listed" according to their historic significance. The Bath plant is currently designated a Grade 2 building, which allows for exterior modifications. Because the building is already perceived as having some historic and aesthetic significance, it is at some risk of being redesignated Grade 1. Such a classification would freeze forever the building's fluid facade in a particular configuration, a strange fate for Herman Miller's original indeterminate building.

Three ideas, linked

Almost everyone at Herman Miller is in love with Marigold. Almost unanimously, they express their satisfaction with what the company was able to accomplish at the formerly run-down property. But why? "I think that one of the things that Marigold shows is quality," says Hugh De Pree. "It shows its excellence. It sends a message to the people who come in there, and the message is, 'If you are going to do something, do it really, really well.'"

"That's one of the things the De Prees have instilled in me," says Gord Nagelkirk. "If it's worth doing, *do it right.* Quality of workmanship, quality of materials, quality of architecture—it's all very, very important."

"I think we learned over the years that good design not only wears well, it's also very cost effective."

Do it right, and *do it right the first time.* "I think we learned over the years that good design not only wears well, it's also very cost effective," comments

Tom Wolterink. "If it's done right the first time, you don't have to do it over. And you get more publicity from good design than you could ever get with advertising dollars. We got more publicity from the Bath plant than we could have ever bought, and it cost maybe an extra buck a square foot to do it right."

Do it right, do it right the first time, and *be tolerant of mistakes.* Just when the windows for the Design Yard were being ordered, the Environmental Protection Agency decided to ban the particular preservative to be used in the windows. Somehow, a shipment of windows was installed at the Design Yard with no preservatives (or perhaps inadequate preservatives) in them. Soon the windows were rotting away at an alarming rate. It became clear that the windows would have to be replaced, an expensive proposition.

At first, fingers began to be pointed, and "if only's" began to be hurled. This wouldn't have been quite so serious, if only the windows had been treated properly. This wouldn't have been quite so serious if only architect Jeff Scherer had detailed a drip cap that would have shunted water away from the windows. There might have been such a detail, if only the budget established by Herman Miller hadn't been so tight.

Eventually it became clear that no single person or company was at fault. This kind of mistake (although very expensive, and deplored by all parties) was almost inevitable, given the complexity and high goals of the project, the overall success of which more than justified forgiveness.

Had there been no such mistakes, suggests John Stivers, Herman Miller and Jeff Scherer might justifiably be faulted for having too limited a vision and taking too few risks. "Look," Stivers comments, reflecting back on this episode, "if you don't push your design team to the limit and get them to make at least one mistake, you probably haven't gotten all their ideas. So we are very tolerant of mistakes."

"Yes, they are," confirms Scherer, noting that all three parties to the debate agreed finally to contribute to its solution. "And that tolerance makes for a terrific client."

"If you don't push your design team to the limit, and get them to make at least one mistake, you probably haven't gotten all their ideas."

The Design Yard

The Midwest Distribution Center

in 1985, Herman Miller decided to combine all of its design and development-related activities, then scattered in four different buildings, in one facility. Numerous alternatives, including the rehabilitation of existing historic structures, were considered. Finally, the company decided to build a new complex on a 40-acre rural site in Holland, Michigan, not far from the Seating Plant.

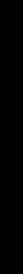

Minneapolis-based architects Meyer, Scherer & Rockcastle (MS&R) were selected to design the new facility. Jeffrey A. Scherer, partner in charge of the project, was already well known to Herman Miller. He had worked with Nicholas Grimshaw on the Bath facility and had subsequently served on the company's Strategic Product Planning Group. "He has," as Herman Miller senior vice president Thomas C. Pratt once noted, "a unique ability to become part of the larger corporate family—a kindred spirit dedicated to developing good ideas, whether his or someone else's." [12]

The Design Yard master plan

Two "outbuildings" at the Design Yard

Officially completed in June, 1989, MS&R's design has sparked controversy. Critics have objected to its fairly literal evocation of a Midwestern farmyard. (But this, the facility's proponents respond, is a positive connotation. Like the schoolyard and the shipyard, the farmyard is a place where learning and work have coexisted productively.) Others have argued that the facility's effort to extend Herman Miller's tradition of "indeterminate" architecture from a single building to an entire complex of buildings doesn't work. Nevertheless, the complex won a citation from *Progressive Architecture* magazine as one of the top 15 designs of 1988, and among Herman Miller's workforce, it is today one of the company's most popular facilities.

Impromptu basketball court at the Design Yard

The Midwest Distribution Center

Like the Design Yard, the Midwest Distribution Center grew out of a need to consolidate activities—in this case, warehousing and distribution. In the 1980s, Herman Miller shipped orders from seven different West Michigan buildings, creating logistical problems, partial shipments, and delayed payments. Consolidation, first considered in the late 1970s, was a pressing need by 1988.

Settling on an appropriate design for a new distribution center, however, was no simple process. Herman Miller's board of directors vetoed the first plan—for a pre-engineered building, which would have been inexpensive and anonymous. Subsequently, local architects Bede Van Dyke and David VerBurg designed a 355,000-square-foot facility, situated on a 161-acre site in Holland.

The building's H-shaped design not only facilitated movement of goods from truck to truck, but also allowed for 19,000 square feet of glass, making the facility surprisingly bright and cheerful. Since 1989, in fact, Herman Miller has held its annual stockholders' meeting in the new building.

The Midwest Distribution Center

"Architecture is the art," wrote John Ruskin in 1849 in his magisterial *The Seven Lamps of Architecture*, "which so disposes and adorns the edifices raised by man, for whatsoever uses, that the sight of them may contribute to his mental health, power, and pleasure."

Like many other arts, the art of architecture since Ruskin's day has become infinitely more complicated. But his notion of the measures of good architecture—mental health, empowerment, and pleasure—still pertains today.

Ruskin's vision was essentially a moral one. Its moral quality helps it endure, and it speaks to the architecture of the contemporary workplace. It also gives Ruskin's pronouncement pertinence to Herman Miller's story. Early in the company's history, Herman Miller benefited from people who gathered in their approach to work three things: a strong sense of moral purpose, a relentless pragmatism, and an abiding commitment to the primacy of design. In the intersections they found, they built an unusual and successful business.

Over subsequent years, like any other organization fortunate enough to survive seventy years, Herman Miller has changed greatly, believing— to paraphrase Carl Frost, consultant and teacher to Herman Miller for over 40 years—that change is the only way to become what you are not now. During those years, architecture has been a means for self-understanding and corporate change. It continues to be so. Why else would the company produce manifestos on architecture every five years or so since 1972?

Herman Miller's experience suggests that architecture, the most concrete of the arts, must stretch itself to accommodate the unpredictable. Hence Herman Miller's focus on the indeterminate building. For many reasons, indeterminacy is hard to achieve. It is even harder to exploit. Sometimes the building is ready and the people are not. The moveable bathroom pods at the Bath building never move. They could, but they don't.

Paradoxically, architecture is also called upon to reinforce tradition and to guard against change. Businesses and organizations change, markets change, product lines come and go. Amid this tide of change, Herman Miller asks that its architecture be timeless in design. This drive for timelessness makes intuitive sense but is extremely difficult to embody in architecture. A client with a zeal for the timeless can drive even the best of architects crazy.

Whereas Ruskin lists mental health, power, and pleasure, philosopher Friedrich Hegel points to spirit as a touchstone for architecture. The whole end of architecture, he wrote in his voluminous *Philosophy of Fine Art*,

Architecture has been a means for self-understanding and corporate change. It continues to be so.

Paradoxically, architecture is also called upon to reinforce tradition and to guard against change.

lies "in so elaborating the external material of inorganic nature that the same becomes intimately connected with spirit as an artistic and external environment." Hegel's "spirit"—his *geist*—might today be translated as "beliefs." Herman Miller expects its beliefs about people, organizations, and work to be made manifest in its buildings. Graphic designer Steve Frykholm explains, "There is just a certain kind of behavior here—the way we manage, the way we do things. There is a trust and respect for the talent and the contributions that everybody makes to the whole."

The trust and respect for people that Herman Miller expects to see embodied in its buildings extends to the architects with whom Herman Miller has built relationships. That may be the central message behind the story of Herman Miller and its architecture: Good architecture results from the healthy relationship between a client and an architect trying to do good together. How to build that relationship, and how to determine exactly what "doing good" is—those must depend on the client, the architect, and the job.

In reviewing the trail of documents and oral histories that has accumulated over the years, we can easily see that the people at Herman Miller have struggled in their efforts to do good. They haven't agreed unanimously on what "good architecture" or "good design" means; they know that it's critically important. They certainly haven't agreed on how to transmit these important undefinables; they all agree that perpetuating them is necessary. Vern Poest, former chief financial officer, puts the challenge this way: "Well, we've talked about how to leave a legacy and how to transfer whatever we had, whatever they were—feelings about honesty, integrity, excellence, good design gets thrown in there somehow. When I try to define 'good design,' I can't. Transferring something you can't define is difficult." Yes, it is, and the struggle is not likely to end soon.

Most at Herman Miller agree, at least, that architecture is one way to define the undefinable, embody it, and transmit it. The failure to seize this opportunity, to pole-vault over the mundane and distracting issues of budgets, bricks, and mortar into the issues that sustain or subvert a human organization, is a huge failure indeed.

An architect recently asked a senior Herman Miller executive what the biggest challenge would be for architects in the future. "Finding good clients," came the answer.

How can Herman Miller or any other corporation become a better client for architecture and thereby sustain, rather than diminish, itself? Some concrete suggestions emerge from the Herman Miller experience: know what you believe in, be ready to learn, acknowledge your debts, proceed sensibly, and admit in advance that there will be mistakes.

Good architecture results from the healthy relationship between a client and an architect trying to do good together.

How can a company become a better client for architecture, and thereby sustain, rather than diminish, itself?

The more elusive and important answers lie somewhere in the ground of faith—that is, faith in the talents and abilities of other people; and faith that to put up a good building is to do something worthwhile.

We have argued that the first step is to determine the spirit of the place and organization. What kind of a company is it that wants to put up a building? What kind of a company do the people who work there want it to become? If you walked the halls of Herman Miller, past one-on-ones and work-team conferences, you would actually hear these questions being asked. You would hear tentative answers being hazarded, explored, reworked, and tried on for size. You might well be tempted to ask, "Why does that company worry so much about that stuff?"

Understanding the nature of an organization and fathoming its reasons for being, involves hard questions about goals and results. Which is which? At Herman Miller, people say that profits (necessary as they are) come as a result of doing other things right. Profits are a result, rather than a goal. When it comes to architecture, such a distinction seems to make for a better client. Can a company really chart a course that leads directly to a building that heals, empowers, and pleases? Herman Miller would say no; it's better to focus on a process—building a healthy, challenging relationship with an architect—and allow good results to come out of that process.

Understanding the nature of an organization involves hard questions about goals and results.

"Winning an architectural award" is certainly one goal. If a company sets its sights on an award, it may be unlucky enough to win one. We say unlucky because the building that results from such a goal may well be rootless and flawed. And in the long run, buildings that set out to be inexpensive often cost inestimably more (in terms of time, effort, and money) than the builders ever dreamed of spending. Buildings that set out to be monuments to an architect's or a CEO's ego often achieve that goal—but little else. Herman Miller's Bath building won one of the most prestigious awards for European architecture. Why? Because a highly talented architect and an educated client built first a healthy relationship, because client and architect fully explored the larger context, because awards and embodiments of ego were judged to be ephemeral.

Buildings that set out to be monuments to an architect's or a CEO's ego often achieve that goal— but little else.

Being a good client for architecture, in Herman Miller's experience, comes down to setting the right goals, making conscious choices, and articulating high expectations. Perhaps the key word is "choice." More than one of Herman Miller's architects uses "editing" as a synonym for choosing. Clients have choices where they may not even see them. Very little in architecture is inevitable. No one forces a company to cover a perfectly good cornfield with asphalt and buildings. That's a choice.

Clients have choices. Very little in architecture is inevitable.

As architect Quincy Jones once said to Max De Pree about architecture, "There are a hundred ways to skin a cat. My job is to find a way that makes us both happy." By diligently trying to define its choices—and by hiring architects with a predisposition to search for choices—Herman Miller makes itself a better client.

In *Leadership Jazz*, Max De Pree tells the story of John Deere's headquarters building, designed by Eero Saarinen and John Dinkeloo. The two architects brought to chairman and CEO Bill Hewitt a design for the building, which was to be built in the woods outside Moline, Illinois. Hewitt told them that their design was a fine one, but that he had expected something a little more *inspired*. The architects went away no doubt chastened and chagrined, but they returned with what all agreed was a dramatically better design. (The new design employed a new kind of steel to achieve a special sympathy with the oak trees on the site.) The client, finding choices, raised the ante. The game was more exciting, and the pot more worth winning.

Like Bill Hewitt, Herman Miller has expected its architects to be thinkers and spokespeople for a particular point of view. It expects them to bring to a project a philosophy of their own. Nick Grimshaw brought to the Bath project an informed sense of history and context, as well as strong ideas about form and function. Jeff Scherer (who trained with Grimshaw) brought to the Design Yard an intimate knowledge of the Midwest, its geography and ethos; his point of view shaped the buildings as much as, if not more than, Herman Miller's functional requirements.

One way to think about choices and expectations is to ask questions. The more peculiar the question, the better. We've mentioned some of the strange questions that people at Herman Miller ask themselves. Some others might be: Do you look at beauty as a choice? Do you look at your organization's buildings as an investment in the spiritual life of a community? What is the connection for you between architecture and a concept of persons? Do you believe that architecture expresses philosophy? Are buildings for you a way of doing what you say—of walking the talk, as the phrase goes? Can an architect teach you something about yourself and your organization? Would you want an architect to design your financial strategy? (Is your CFO designing your building?) Will your new building serve the spirit of the people who will work there as attentively as it will cater to the machinery within it? Over time, does a thoughtful user improve a building?

> One way to think about choices and expectations is to ask questions. The more peculiar the question, the better.

Of course, the questions which you and your organization come up with must be your own. True, question-shaping takes a little time. But it's far better to spend time dreaming up and pondering these questions in advance than to grumble about an unsuccessful building for 10, 20, 50, or 100 years. That's a lot of time.

A last critical capacity of a good client is judgment. Good judgment has helped Herman Miller build good buildings. Once again, we'll describe the foundation of this judgment: moral purpose, a relentless pragmatism, and an abiding commitment to the primacy of design. Each of these traits helps Herman Miller—both in investing its architects as the company's leaders and teachers, and also in challenging their teachings in productive ways.

We've told a story of a company and its architecture: its structure of beliefs, and its beliefs about structures. Underneath it all, the idea seems to be the thing. This is one of the most striking aspects about talking with Herman Miller's architects: They are incessant teachers. They love ideas and are extremely generous with them. They need very little prompting to launch into an impromptu seminar. They are difficult to muzzle. More power to them.

Good architects, like all imaginative people, threaten the status quo and question received wisdom. Like individuals, organizations with a strong sense of who they are and what they are about welcome such questioning. Their spiritual muscle tone improves with the exercise of finding answers. In contrast, the insecure organization becomes defensive, sealed off, and flabby.

Architects, too, can get flabby, with consequences that are just as serious. Buckminster Fuller once asked an odd question, as he flew over a new building in a helicopter. Also in the helicopter was the facility's architect, who seemed to know all there was to know about the building.

"How much does it weigh?" Fuller asked the architect.

For client and architect—for the architecture that brings them together—an odd question with no easy answer may be a wonderful starting point.

Rocklin

Rocklin

Like Herman Miller's plant in Roswell, Georgia, the Rocklin facility (formally the "Western Region Facility") grew out of the company's "rapid response" policy for filling customers' orders. The need, as perceived in the early 1980s, was for a manufacturing and warehousing facility that would allow overnight delivery to all West Coast markets, and also simplify the manufacturing and shipping of products destined for Asian markets.

Site plan

The site chosen was a hilly 156-acre tract in Rocklin, California, 21 miles northeast of Sacramento. The architectural firm selected was Venice, California-based Frank O. Gehry & Associates, and Peter Walker was hired as landscape architect. Frank Gehry was an interesting choice. One of the nation's leading architects, he was celebrated for, among other things, his creative use of common building materials.

Pergola at the Rocklin building

Construction began in the fall of 1986 on the first 300,000 square feet of a planned 750,000-square-foot facility. The building employed low-cost materials, such as galvanized metal; but it still managed to achieve dramatic effect, in part as a result of a 75-foot-tall, copper-clad pergola in the center of the structure.

Also notable at Rocklin was Gehry's collaboration with Stanley Tigerman, a Chicago-based architect whose firm (Tigerman Fugman McCurry Architects) had previously helped design Herman Miller's Chicago showroom at the Merchandise Mart. Tigerman designed a small, temple-like building in the center of the Rocklin facility, used as a meeting area, and this smaller structure helps orient visitors and establish a human scale, balancing Gehry's oversized trellis.

Rocklin has been well received. In November 1989, *Landscape Architecture* magazine gave the facility an "honor award" for its context-sensitive landscaping. And early in 1991, Rocklin received the most prestigious of awards for a work of architecture in the US: an Honor Award for Design Excellence from the American Institute of Architects.

The meeting area and courtyard at Rocklin.

The site at Rocklin, California

Notes

Chapter 1

Unless otherwise noted, all quoted material comes from interviews conducted by the authors.

1. See, for example, Robert Levering, Milton Moskowitz, and Michael Katz, *The 100 Best Companies to Work for in America.*

2. "Architect's Statement," by Laurence Booth of Booth/Hansen & Associates, in the *Master Plan for Facility Development* for the Grandville, Michigan, facility.

3. For more detail and for a business perspective on Herman Miller and architecture, see *Fortune* magazine (June 15, 1981), p. 174.

4. *Architecture Factbook: Industry Statistics* (New York: The American Institute of Architects, 1990), p. 6.

5. Robert Gutman, *Architectural Practice: A Critical View* (New York: Princeton Architectural Press, 1988), p. 8.

6. See *Building Design & Construction* (July 1992), p. 28.

7. *Architectural Factbook*, p. 7.

8. Wolfgang F.E. Preiser, Jacqueline C. Vischer, and Edward T. White, eds., *Design Intervention: Toward a More Humane Architecture* (New York: Van Nostrand Reinhold, 1991), p. 303.

9. Quoted in "A Non-precious Image," *Progressive Architecture* (February 1990).

10. Ted Reed, "Herman Miller pioneers design, management," *Sacramento Bee* (May 25, 1986).

11. An undated letter from S. Jay Neyland III, senior vice president of Caudill Rowlett Scott, to D.J. De Pree.

12. *Herman Miller Memo*, (August 1960).

13. Quoted in Jacqueline C. Vischer's epilogue to *Design Intervention: Toward a More Humane Architecture*, p. 363.

14. *Design Intervention: Toward a More Humane Architecture*, p. 303.

15. *Ibid.*, p. 306.

16. "Building Types Study 697/The New Workplace," *Architectural Record* (June 1992), p. 69.

17. *Ibid.*, p. 120.

18. D.J. De Pree, writing in *Twice A Month* (July 1948), an internal newsletter.

19. *Headlines* (1/27/69), an internal newsletter.

Chapter 2

1. Hugh De Pree, *Business as Unusual* (Zeeland, Michigan: Herman Miller Inc., 1986), p. 1.

2. From a 10/15/85 interview.

3. Hugh De Pree, p. 27.

4. *Ibid.*, p. 117.

5. From a 10/15/85 interview.

6. Memo (7/6/77) to HMI's Board of Directors

Chapter 3

1. Letter (5/30/80) from Walters and Max De Pree to Wolterink.

2. See, for example, *Financial World* (December 1-5, 1981), p. 57, for the distinctions among the various kinds of construction firms.

3. From Scherer's notes for a lecture.

4. "Profiting by good design," *Interiors* (March 1981), p. 87.

5. Memo (4/25/85) from Pratt to Wolterink.

6. From Kathy Pruden's memo summarizing the 6/6/80 programming session with CRS.

7. From a 10/15/85 interview.

8. Letter (9/11/78) from John B. Hackler to Tom Wolterink.

9. Frank Gehry interview with Pratt.

10. *Twice a Month* (11/26/47).

Chapter 4

1. Frank O. Gehry, the "Master Plan Proposal for the Western Regional Facility" (June 1986).

2. O/I Facility Strategy Overview (August 15, 1978) p. 2.

3. *Headlines* (4/25/57).

4. D.J. De Pree interview with William Houseman.

5. *Ibid.*

6. *Architectural Record* (October 1981), p. 112.

7. Memo (4/27/81) to Phil Strengholt regarding the "Super Room for Holland Manufacturing— East Mezzanine."

8. From the agenda for a 10/16/86 "Preliminary Design Development Review Meeting," p. 2.

9. From a 1988 interview with John Stivers, Julie Christiansen Stivers, and Tom Pratt.

10. Bath brief.

11. *Building Design & Construction* (March 1984), p. 171.

12. George Nelson interviewed by Studs Terkel and Marty Robinson.

13. From a June 1972 "Herman Miller Direction Statement."

14. Maeve Slavin, "Power Play in Michigan," *Interiors* (March 1983).

15. "The Indeterminate Building Takes Shape," *Architectural Record* (January 1983), p. 123.

16. *Connections* (May 1989), an employee newsletter, p. 4.

17. Robert B. Rosen, *Healthy Companies: A human resources approach*, (An AMA Management briefing), p. 43.

18. From D.J. De Pree's 1980 interview with Ralph Caplan.

19. Steve Frykholm, *Perspective* (December 1985), p. 2.

20. "City on a Hill," *Architectural Record* (January 1990).

21. "Design Yard fits Herman Miller image," *Holland Sentinel* (September 17, 1989), p. 14.

22. "Draft program for Design Facility" (7/1/85).

23. "The Architecture of Nick Grimshaw, Book 2: Process," (Nicholas Grimshaw & Partners), p. 21.

24. *Headlines* (1/27/61).

25. HMI brochure entitled "Resolution to the shareholders of Herman Miller in memory of Bill Caudill."

Chapter 5

1. O/I Facility Strategy Overview (August 15, 1978), p. 2.

2. "Earthwork begins for Sacramento facility," *Perspective* (Fall 1986).

3. "Herman Miller picks site by Sacramento," *Fresno Bee* (5/29/86), p. AA2.

4. Memo (6/80) from Kathy Pruden summarizing the 6/6/80-6/8/80 programming sessions for Building B.

5. From *Master Plan and first phase of new construction*, prepared by A. Quincy Jones, F.A.I.A. and Associates, Architects, Inc., and Newhof and Winer, Inc., consulting engineers (December 1974), p. 5.

6. "William W. Caudill: Founder and 'Spiritual Leader' of CRS," *Architecture* (August 1983), p. 41.

7. Memo (9/17/84) from John Stivers to Gary Miller.

8. Memo (9/19/80) from Tom Wolterink to John Stivers.

9. Frank Gehry interview with Bill Houseman.

10. Memo (1/29/70) from Dick Ruch to Ed Nagelkirk, Tony Muiderman, and Vern Poest.

11. Memo (5/15/79) from John Stivers to Gord Nagelkirk.

12. Memo (12/2/79) from George Cary to Joe Schwartz.

13. *Connections* (May 1989), p. 4.

Chapter 6

1. *Twice a Month* (4/26/54).

2. Memo (1/13/81) from Jim Ries to various insiders.

3. William Caudill, *Perspective* (October 1979), quoting from Philip P. Crosby's *Quality is Free*.

4. Memo (8/22/79) from Jim Ries to Dick Ruch.

5. Memo (1/14/81) from CRS to John Stivers, summarizing the meetings on 1/8/81 and 1/9/81.

6. Memo (8/4/81) from Jim Hosta to Jim Ries.

7. Memo (6/2/69) from Dick Ruch to Ed Nagelkirk, Tony Muiderman, and Vern Poest.

8. *RIBA Journal* (September 1983).

9. Letter (10/30/79) from insurance agent to Herman Miller.

10. Memo (2/4/82) from Jim Ries to Phil Strengholt.

11. Letter (3/30/80) from Owens-Ames-Kimball Co. to vendor.

12. Letter (10/3/88) from Tom Pratt to Ed Braman of Braman & Nelson, Inc., recommending Scherer to B & N.

Index

Herman Miller Inc.:
Buildings and Beliefs
was designed and produced
on a Macintosh computer by
Kohn Cruikshank Inc, Boston.
The typefaces used in this
book are Adobe Garamond,
Adobe Garamond Oldstyle
and Frutiger. The paper is
Mitsubishi 157 gm. Matte Art.
The book was printed and
bound in Hong Kong through
Palace Press International,
San Francisco.